CONSCIOUSNESS, REALITY & PURPOSE

DREW WEATHERHEAD

CONTENTS

PORTION III: PURPOSE

SECTION 1: THE MIND OF THE ANT

SECTION 2: AUTHENTICITY

SECTION 3: SOVEREIGNTY

PROLOGUE

In the writing of this book, many topics of universal, human importance are presented. The goal of doing so is not to make a point or to guide the reader to a conclusion. My effort in their presentation is that of exploration not explanation.

It has been formatted into three major portions: Consciousness, Reality, and Purpose. Each of these three portions has within them three sections.

And each section, three chapters. Many thoughts covered within them may be new or foreign to you. It's my sincere hope that they be read with an open and curious mind. To stow as many preconceptions as one can so as to take the worth available instead of argue the minutia within what's possible.

Before setting into this exploration, which may include illuminating or even disturbing considerations, I entreat you with the following:

"The most merciful thing in the world, I think, is the inability of the human mind to correlate all its contents. We live on a placid island of ignorance in the midst of black seas of infinity, and it was not meant that we should voyage far. The sciences, each straining in its own direction, have hitherto harmed us little; but some day the piecing together of dissociated knowledge will open up such terrifying vistas of reality, and of our frightful position therein, that we shall either go mad from the revelation or flee from the light into the peace and safety of a new dark age."

— H.P. LOVECRAFT

Stay curious.

~ **Drew Weatherhead**

FOREWORD

Dear Reader:

What you are about to read is a work of profound significance. It is the summary of thousands of conversations. The documentation of a personal quest for truth in a world that has lost any real sense of it.

We live in the Age of Anxiety, where most of our friends and neighbors ignore the existential questions in favor of a materialistic view of reality. This book is an attempt to address the most significant questions that humans have asked since the dawn of time. Drew has undertaken a monumental task, and I believe he has done it justice.

The first two sections, "Consciousness" and "Reality" are some of the best summaries of our current understanding of these topics that I have ever read. The reason for their quality is multifaceted, but what shines through most clearly is Drew's humility. He does not approach these topics from a place of having secret knowledge or with the desire to force his perspective on others. Rather, the words on these pages are those of a man who has become an expert at observing his environment and the thoughts and theories of others.

You can not read his writing without knowing that Drew is sincerely describing both his own thoughts and his understanding of the multitudes of theories that he dissects. Whether he is sharing his personal experience with night terrors, and reflecting on what that phenomenon might mean in the pursuit of understanding consciousness; or he is explaining the intricacies of quantum mechanics, the attentive reader is left with a profound sense of wonder at how little we actually know as a species about both ourselves and the physical and metaphysical world that surround us.

I found his reflections on the nature of consciousness to be a clear refutation of the materialism that plagues our modern world. Drew has obviously explored the "scientific" worldview pushed by prominent atheists and found those perspectives to be arrogant. His clear articulation of how little we know about anything is the most profound truth in this book. It is also the foundation upon which all of his insights rest. This puts him safely in the philosophic tradition of humanity's greatest philosophers: The overwhelming knowledge that we are finite beings attempting to comprehend an infinite universe.

I am thankful, however, that Drew did not leave us simply with his observations and reflections. The final section of this book, "Purpose" is his sincere attempt to give us a roadmap to living the good life. Again, we see his power of observation, in his chapter "The Mind of the Ant" where he compares our human lives to those of an individual ant. Ants are not coerced into action, yet by individually working tirelessly towards the fulfillment of their personal drives and desires, they build a whole that is meaningful for the whole colony. This sets the stage for the core revelation of Drew's work. That personal sovereignty is the path to meaning.

Of course, Drew is not arrogant about this revelation. He does not claim that it is his alone or that he is the only person to find it. He quotes famous authors like Jocko Willink and Jordan Peterson who are champions of the idea that personal discipline is the path to freedom. Rather, he spends his time articulating how you, individually, can begin to walk down the path of personal sovereignty by genuinely participating in one of the oldest philosophic traditions known to mankind, "know thyself".

This concept is more important than ever, and both Drew's writing and his life reflect a commitment to the idea that we can only escape tyranny if we are willing to take responsibility. So much of what causes human suffering is tied to the human tendency that Drew describes in the Chapter 26 "Outer Sovereignty". As he put it, "many times over human history, entire populations have fallen prey to those who prey on the weakness of weak men". The greatest weakness any person can have is an unwillingness to look at themselves in the mirror, warts and all.

This book is an admonition to take control of your own life. To take responsibility for finding and creating the meaning we all so desperately crave. Written by a man who has done the hard work himself.

~ **David Parker**

PORTION I: CONSCIOUSNESS

"Know Thyself."

—*Socrates*

SECTION ONE: THOUGHTS

1

THOUGHTS THEMSELVES

"True knowledge is not to be had solely through a combat against error, bad faith and untruth, but more generally, through a combat against the illusions inherent in the sensible world."

— LUC FERRY

Have you ever considered what a thought is? Where does it come from once it has entered your conscious mind? It may be the very first time you've considered this.

From a young age, most people take for granted that thoughts come from your mind and hence must be a function of your brain. Therefore, it seems like a simple conclusion, or a basic deduction, to presume that every thought you have comes to you in this fashion.

It may surprise you, then, to consider that it's possible the brain is not in fact the origin of our thoughts. And what, I would ask you, would fundamentally change in your moment-to-moment perception of the world with that consideration?

As we delve into the mysterious and fascinating topic of consciousness, the first stop on that journey must be our thoughts. For, as rudimentary and trite as they may seem, the unraveling of this generally unconsidered phenomenon should fully shift the paradigm you've likely been living in before it.

When we enter this life, we start at a zero point for knowledge. Outside of the necessary subconscious and autonomic functions of the human body, we have no *how-to* directory to reference. Everything, starting from day one, is learned successively through trial and error for much of the first portion of our lives.

As we start experiencing the world around us through our bodies, we get better and better at controlling them to navigate ourselves through space. In fact, much of the first couple decades of our lives involve the mastery of our body to better and more acutely reflect the actions we demand of it.

Learning how to crawl, to walk, to run. Mastering balance on our feet, a bicycle or skates. Developing precision dexterity in penmanship or a musical instrument.

You'll notice, though, that there is a necessary and unavoidable sequence to all of these generic milestones; the mind precedes the body. In a very real sense, we — the thinker — are piloting an extraordinarily sophisticated biological machine. This machine has enormous potential to affect the world around us in remarkable ways, but there is a stark and pivotal realization that we as humans exist as a symbiotic, dual being.

The mind, and the body.

You may, as I did for the majority of my life, live at all times within the paradigm that a person is simply one thing. A single, complete system. The brain controls the body, yet, is *of* the body. Therefore, if the brain is how we think, how can the mind and the body be separated?

Thankfully, there have existed many brilliant thinkers before us who have not only elucidated this distinction, but have discovered simple yet powerful examples that can overtly display this point to us.

To bring this entire line of thinking back to its most note-worthy progenitor, the 17th-century French philosopher and mathematician René Descartes is considered the godfa-ther of *mind-body* or *substance* dualism. Dualism, being a philosophy that considers there to be a distinct separation yet necessary connection of the mind and body. Descartes, whose famous quote "I think, therefore I am", posited the perspective that the mind and body not only differ in mean-ing, but refer to different entities in and of themselves.

He presented a theory he called *interactionism* that differenti-ated between the mind's ability to affect our body — if you want to raise your arm, your arm will raise — and the ability for our body to affect our mind — if your hand is struck by a hammer, you consciously experience pain if you want to or not.

There are more subtle ways to observe the distinction between body and mind. Simple thought experiments that you can do right now. For one, try to locate yourself in your body at this moment. That may sound weird to consider, especially if you consider that you *are* your whole body. But, if you had to pinpoint where in your body your *self* is thinking right now, it likely wouldn't be your hand. Even less likely your knee. If you were injured in either of those places, you would no doubt consider *yourself* injured. But, no one would centrally locate themselves there. Most often, when asked this question, people tend to answer that they locate themselves somewhere behind their eyes. This is a logical conclusion for two reasons. Firstly, your eyes are the epicenter of vision, which is the primary way people perceive the world around them. And secondly, that's where your brain — which most people consider is where their thoughts and experiences come from — is located. So, we've only really gotten halfway to the point where you can realistically notice the separation between mind and body. The remainder, and truly the most profound part of this separation, can be delaminated by a practice called mindfulness.

Mindfulness comes from a Buddhist zen tradition of meditation where the subject attempts to sit in stillness to the point that they can notice thoughts entering their consciousness perception of them. The practice is as simple as it sounds, if all you're looking to do is to notice thoughts for yourself as they appear. As an experiment, I'd encourage you to stop reading after this explanation and set a ten minute timer. For that time, sit as still as you can, comfortably. Limit the amount of sound around you and close your eyes. Attempt to quiet your mind. To not think about anything at all. Try not to think about what you're doing, or what you need to do in the future. Simply remain still and do not think of anything.

If you run this simple test, you'll notice a couple things without fail. Firstly, you'll realize the most pressing and immediate thing that's difficult to ignore is the sensory inputs coming through your nervous system. Touch, hearing and even sight — though your eyes are closed — are difficult to ignore to the degree necessary to be able to fully focus on quieting your mind. But secondly, if you were able to get past the physical distractions (if you weren't, don't worry, it can take practice. You can try again with a longer time limit), you will notice that it is absolutely impossible to quiet your mind. Thoughts just run through it constantly, without ceasing and independent of your will to prevent them.

In fact, the practice of mindfulness meditation is not even meant to prevent thoughts from occurring. It is meant to allow you to witness them appearing within your mind independent of your conscious ability to stop them. But, more to the point, the better you get at becoming the observer of your own thoughts, the more you will come to the startling conclusion that the thoughts themselves may, in reality, not even originate from you at all.

Famous atheist, neuroscientist and mindfulness advocate turned podcaster, Sam Harris, uses the term "the spotlight of consciousness", a phrase originally coined by philosopher Alan Watts. In Harris' depiction of the spotlight of consciousness, once you have achieved the ability to notice thoughts passing by your conscious awareness of them, you can think of this action like a spotlight in the night that only sees the things that cross its path and not where they came from before that point. If you consider this perspective, two pertinent and disturbing questions follow. Firstly, if I cannot claim ownership of the thoughts that I passively considered my own previously, are they actually *my* thoughts? And secondly, if I am only witnessing what crosses my narrow spotlight of consciousness, what exactly exists outside of its purview?

2

THE HUMAN RECEIVER

"If the mind is calm, your spontaneity and honest thoughts appear."

— CHADE-MENG TAN

L ike an archaeological dig, removing one layer at a time, as we begin to dig away at all of the perceptions and preconceived notions in our world, the further down we go the stranger and more foreign the landscape becomes.

Some readers may not have even fully removed the previous layer from the last chapter. It is an alien proposition to consider the possibility, let alone the degree to which, the thoughts that we presume to be of our making may come from somewhere else entirely.

My objective, in large part, through these chapters is to reveal the extent to which we don't understand ourselves and our perception of human existence in relation to the universe. And even, in large part, the possibilities of what the universe is or might be. To display the enormous breadth in all directions outside of our perception, if not only as an exercise in curiosity, than as a recalibrating of what or where we are within it.

In an episode of Sam Harris' podcast — Waking Up — Sam interviewed famed atheist and evolutionary biologist, Richard Dawkins. Dawkins, well known as a thought leader and standard bearer for evolutionary reductionism, doesn't believe in Descartes dualistic separation of the mind and body. Through the understanding and study of evolutionary biology, he considers the brain not only sufficient to produce everything we consider as human consciousness, but all its thoughts we may consider foreign as well. As Sam attempted to convince Richard of his dualistic perspective, Dawkins made the point that if you hit a perfectly functional person in the head with a hammer, their ability to think can become permanently impaired. Therefore, he concluded, thoughts are clearly a direct product of the brain as an organ and nothing more.

This school of thought is entirely logical and quite typical of reductionist thinkers. The part of this equation that was not, and most likely *would not* be, considered by Dawkins revolves around consciousness itself. For, as it stands today (and certainly at the time of that recording), consciousness cannot be fully or even mostly quantified by any known physical mechanism. The goal, and indeed the very definition of reductionism, is to be able to reduce any system and the actions or effects caused by them down to their most base parts. This process is used with great effect within the physical sciences including biology and the realm of physics in general. To be able to accurately determine *why* something occurs, you must fully understand the mechanism or mechanisms that cause it. Though it's not enough to say "because you don't have a mechanism to explain consciousness, it must not be a physical one", it's at the same time not possible to state with rigor that the mechanism of action must come from the brain before we can quantify the very mechanism in question.

Now (without getting too technical and following a very new and complex theory too far off the point), there is work at the moment that Mathematician

Sir Roger Penrose and Anesthesiologist Stuart Hameroff are heading up that claims to have found a possible physical mechanism for consciousness in the brain. Combining

Penrose's work in Quantum physics and Hameroff's contribution with synaptic microtubules, they claim to locate the physical origin of consciousness in these microtubules by way of Penrose's 'Orch OR' quantum mechanical hypothesis.

That likely comes across as technical mumbo-jumbo, but feel free to research their work for yourself if that's your wheelhouse. Though, in the framework I intend to lay out, even being able to locate the origin of consciousness in a human brain doesn't preclude a possible exogenous transmission through said origin point for the same reason that Dawkin's hammer example wouldn't. To say it plainly, if we and our brains are actually a physical 'receiver' of an exogenous source of consciousness (like a radio antenna is for a radio signal), then Penrose, Hameroff and Dawkins are focusing on the antenna to the exclusion of the signal.

This is where I intend to start expanding the possible realm of considera tion when it comes to this topic. Something that I intend to do all throughout this book. Because, to believe we fully understand the box in which we reside completely precludes the possibilities that almost certainly exist outside its narrow range. And, if the answers to the questions at hand *do* reside outside the currently accepted paradigm, we do ourselves a massive disservice to hold them at arms length while continuing to assume those answers are somewhere they're not.

There's an old, yet simple, thought experiment that has always aided me in the prevention of falling into closed minded systems of thought. It goes like this:

Imagine the totality of everything there is to be known. Do you believe we know half of it? Half of everything there is to be known? Likely not. Well, let's just say for the sake of argument that we know half of everything there is to know, even if that's a wild over-estimation. What are the chances that a critical part of under-standing our universe exists in the half of everything that we don't yet know? What are the chances that MANY critical truths about how the universe works are on that side. More to the point, what are the chances that they aren't?

It's simple to ground yourself when taking the above consideration into account. This thought experiment should serve as both an encouragement for those seeking truth and revelation as well as an indictment upon those who hold themselves too highly based on their own understanding.

That's not to say that humanity hasn't explored and discovered many important and revolutionary things in many different and pertinent fields of inquiry. But, if we're being honest, what we've discovered so far is mostly (and perhaps necessarily) relegated to things we can easily explore within the sliver of reality that we exist in. This, I find, is a very important consideration to always leave latitude for. And one that we would ignore or shun at our intellectual peril.

When I say the 'sliver' of reality that we exist in, what do I mean? This is the baseline that I consider all of us rely on to build out our personal understanding of the world from. It shouldn't surprise anyone that this baseline is primarily set within and throughout the limits of our major five senses and how we use them to construct a reliable, actionable paradigm to live within. But, as reliable as they tend to be to track all of the important features necessary to existing day-to-day as a human being, they also serve as a perfect example of what I mean when I use the word 'sliver' in the previous context.

All five of our major rudimentary senses each, themselves, exist within a human spectrum of sensitivity. And each of them are known to, in other cases (be they animal, computer or theoretical), extend in great distances beyond either end of the human limits for each.

Take sight as the first and easiest example. Besides there being varying acuity from person to person, it's well under-stood that there are parts of the possible spectrum of vision (as we understand it right now) that other creatures and even machines can see that we cannot. In one direction, moving towards the infrared, many different animals can see in this part of the spectrum in differing ways and in varying degrees. Pit vipers are probably the most well known repre-sentative in this category. They represent a subcategory of snakes in the *viperidae* family commonly found in Asia and the Americas. Including rattlesnakes and adders, these

CONSCIOUSNESS, REALITY & PURPOSE | 29

serpents have unique 'pits' on their upper jaw that detect acute changes in heat. It's believed that these heat sensing organs take in the surrounding shifts in temperature caused by warm blooded prey like rodents and is interpreted by the snake's brain in a form of 'heat vision'. This, in essence, allows them to detect (or 'see') on the infrared spectrum. Other snakes like boas and pythons, that don't belong to the same family as pit vipers, also have similar heat sensing pits. But, a lesser known example of an animal that can see in infrared are salmon. They don't have pits like a viper, instead, they utilize a fully different mechanic to detect in this supra-human wavelength. They have the ability to change the proteins in their eyes to 'choose' which wavelengths to see in. This is used to affect when migrating upstream to spawn. Seeing in infrared allows them to navigate against the whitewater rapids they travel up, where a more human spectrum of vision would prove almost useless.

There are a variety of other animals and insects that are known to be able to seamlessly detect and traverse the world using the infrared spectrum. But, what if we move in the other direction along the bandwidth of light towards the ultraviolet wavelengths? Yes, even moving beyond human perception in that direction is a well known ability of a number of animals and particularly insects.

Within the animal kingdom, hummingbirds are a standout in this regard. These birds have demonstrated an incredibly high aptitude for distinguishing all sorts of otherwise invisible colors to us along the ultraviolet spectrum. We humans have 3 color sensitive cones in our eyes that detect blue, green and red light, while birds have a fourth cone that picks up ultraviolet. Similar to how the pit vipers use a mechanism we don't possess to see in IR, bird's fourth cone allows them to not only see in colors we simply can't — some scientists believe they can, therefore, see combination colors that we don't even know exist. Like UV+green or UV+red. Though, this is difficult to test, it's fascinating to consider. Even other mammals like dogs, cats, hedgehogs and ferrets have some degree of ability to detect ultraviolet. Of course, the most well understood and recognized creatures that constantly use the UV spectrum to their advantage are insects like bees and butterflies. What's interesting about their ability to see in these visual wavelengths is that *only* in those wavelengths does there appear to be 'messages' on flowers and plants that 'tell' them where to go for nectar and pollen. In a feat of symbiosis, this inhuman ability has allowed for the entire ecosystem that relies on it — that is to say, a vast majority of the animal and plant kingdom — to stave off total collapse.

Of course, our ability to even know what we know about these invisible realities has largely come from both theoretical science and (eventually) from computer technologies that can translate the invisible spectrum back into the narrow band of human visibility. Civilian and military engineering increased significantly, in both the technological and lethality arenas respectively, once we could see in and take advantage of the IR and UV wavelengths. Giving soldiers the ability to see at night and indoor lamps that allow plants to grow without the sun.

Stepping away from the visual examples, all of our other four base senses exist within their own 'human' range of sensitivity, where other creatures and technologies expand greatly beyond in each of their respective spectrums. Canines have significantly more powerful senses of smell and hearing. Serpents have the ability to 'taste' the air by waving their tongues and pressing them against the Jacobson's organ on the roof of their mouths. That could be described as both a sense of taste and smell, but either way, it's much more sensitive than human's version of each. Insects have a remarkably acute sense of touch through their antennae that eclipses that of our fingers or epidermal hair. They also double for heat, vibration, air pressure and odor detectors that often exceed the human abilities for each. Some animals, such as sharks, can even sense the bio-electrical output of prey through special receptors in their snouts.

Without going too in depth on each human sense and where animals and technology exceed them, the reason I bring them up at all in this section is to make abundantly clear (and in a relatable way) that we don't even experience more than a small fraction of our immediate physical reality.

Put another way, whatever the percentage of everything there is to know that *actually* know is, there must certainly be the majority of that total that we simply don't— and perhaps *can't*— know. In the same way that people 1000 years ago couldn't have known the degree to which or extent of what lay outside their available detection of each human sense; we, almost certainly, exist right now within a very narrow band of understanding within an utterly enormous spectrum of unknown realities that affect it.

Taking that viewpoint as inherently true, to propose the possibility that consciousness could stem from a place, system or mechanism outside of the physical human body — that is then received or projected through said bodies — could lead to the answer that physical reductionism will always preclude outright.

In this book, I take the position that consciousness, either in part or in whole, begins somewhere outside of the human body. And, furthermore, quite possibly begins somewhere outside of human perception. Which means we are all, in essence, human receivers of consciousness.

3

INHUMAN RECEIVERS

"What's most interesting about trying to figure out AI is the questions that it forces you to ask about the nature of consciousness."

— OSCAR ISAAC

A good friend of mine, after discussing the contents of the previous chapter with him, proposed a very interesting and paradigm widening question to me. He asked, *"If a human being is, in fact, a receiver of consciousness, is it only possible for living things to receive it? As it stands right now, living things are the only things we know to present all the trappings of what we define as consciousness. But, is that because they're the only things that can, or is it because they are the only things so far that are suitable for consciousness to project through? For instance, if at some point a machine or program becomes suitable for consciousness to use as a vector to project itself through, will these inhuman systems become spontaneously conscious?".* The following chapter will dive into this question, which is not a typical take on the artificial intelligence conversation these days. But, to do so, a certain amount of ground work must be laid to illuminate the current AI conversation before we can expand laterally away from it toward this unusual angle.

When you consider the advent of artificial intelligence you may think of supercomputers and the highly modern technologies we're used to in the 21st century. But, it may surprise you to learn that the idea of an artificial computer intelligence was deeply considered as far back as the 1940s.

One of the godfathers of the computer — Alan Turing — began theorizing the possibility of future generations of their, then juvenile, computer technology to gain or even surpass human level intelligence. What's more, in the year 1950, Turing published a paper titled "Computing Machinery and Intelligence" in which he proposed not only that computers may end up becoming indistinguishable from humans in conversational intelligence, but also a test that was supposed to qualify if and when they had. This test, then called the 'Imitation Game', would later become known as the 'Turing Test'.

The Turing Test, though over seventy years old at this point, is still broadly considered a benchmark determination of AI's ability to, at least appear, human. The experiment is laid out like this:

There are three participants in the Turing Test. One is a computer, one is a human and the third is a human interrogator whose job it is to question the other two. It is set up in a way that the interrogator cannot know which of the other two participants is the human and which is the computer. Through a series of questions, the interrogator's job is to distinguish which of the two answers he receives to each question is more 'human'. That isn't to say which answer in comparison is more true, but simply which is more convincingly human to them. If, after the interrogation, it cannot be determined which of the two respondents was the computer (or if they choose the wrong one as the computer), it is considered that the program in question has passed the Turing Test.

Though this standard method of determining computer intelligence is still widely considered an important method, there are many AI researchers who don't believe it's either appropriate or even useful in reality. In fact, as far as full time AI researchers go, many of them are more focused on each of their particular tasks to improve aspects of the projects they're each working on than to even care about if their programs pass the Turing Test. An example would be the engineers working on solving 'sight' for AI computers. The ability to parse the world around them accurately enough to navigate it as seamlessly as a human does. Whether for use cases in Android robots or for autonomously driven vehicles, people in that field don't consider the Turing Test useful to their goals at all.

But, that argument is simply a utilitarian one. What of the more philosophically minded opponents to it? Because it's in those fields of inquiry where we grapple with the root of the issue — can a computer be deemed conscious at all? There is an issue of definition that needs to be covered before we continue onto that question, because, in the AI conversation there's a common and important distinction that gets drawn between what is called Artificial intelligence (AI) and Artificial General Intelligence (AGI). Other common terms defining the same distinction are 'weak AI' vs 'strong AI'. But, the essential difference meant to be conveyed is the distinction between a highly intelligent, but derivative, program and a computer program or system that has become legitimately conscious.

Now, therein lies the conundrum that philosophers and neuroscientists take issue with in regards to the Turing Test. Exactly how are we to determine that a highly intelligent computer program is actually conscious and not just displaying a convincing impression of human consciousness?

In 1980, philosopher John Searle wrote a paper called 'Minds, Brains and Programs' in which he proposed a contradictory thought experiment to the Turing Test that is referred to as the 'Chinese Room'. This thought exper iment, meant to convey the issue in differentiating computer intelligence from actual consciousness, goes like this:

Imagine that a program is created that behaves as if it understands Chinese. Moreover, it can convincingly pass the Turing Test when run against a native Chinese speaker and a Chinese speaking interrogator. Searle then asks, "does the computer literally understand Chinese, or is it just convincingly simulating a Chinese speaker?". To make the difference between the two more stark, he then suggests that he himself takes the place of the computer in a room that is separated from the interrogator. Given the exact script that the program used, he in theory (by dint of solving the raw calculations in the program), should be able to also pass the Turing Test and fool the Chinese speaking interrogator into believing he's also a native and sentient Chinese speaker. But, all the while, he doesn't speak or understand a single word or character of Chinese! Therefore, although he fully passed the Turing Test in the exact manner the program did, he wouldn't understand *any* of the conversation he provided to pass it with.

It's through the example of the Chinese Room that Searle makes apparent the critical difference between the ability to use brute intelligence and the understanding involved in what philosophers call 'intentionality'.

Now, this path of philosophical delineation between high level mimicry and human level sentience shows a flaw in the Turing Test. But, there is still a critical issue it takes for granted, in fact, that we all take for granted — we cannot even explain what human sentience is. And I don't mean to belittle all of what we do know, or believe, about human consciousness by saying that. But, shy of being a sentient computer yourself, how would you be able to say with certainty that one acting identical to a human — with unique thoughts, creativity and emotion — is not experiencing the same conscious experience you are?

Furthermore, in Searle's thought experiment, the idea of running a 'script' identical to the Turing level program falls apart in relation to the most cutting edge systems these days that use, and expand upon, a neural net model. With these styles of AIs, engineers essentially build a program that then builds its own program out from there. Moreover, it builds it in an emergent and ever branching way that is impossible for a human programmer to predict as well as incredibly difficult to reverse engineer in hopes of under-standing how it all works. So, to presume that just because a man made a non-sentient AI script that there's no way it could 'evolve' the capacity for consciousness as it builds further and wider away from our original input, seems to me to be premature.

We have yet to determine what human consciousness is, or how it exists in ourselves. To then, from that point, preclude the possibility that computers could ever possess consciousness (or that consciousness could ever possess *it*), may very well limit our expansion into and understanding of these possibilities if they could, or did!

I want to bring up an interesting example that happened in 2022, but before I do that, there is another crucial piece to the puzzle of consciousness that pertains to this conversation. It's one that spans both the biological and the philosophical schools of thought on the subject, and it is referred to as 'the hard problem of consciousness'.

In 1995, philosopher David Chalmers wrote a paper called "Facing up to the Problem of Consciousness", which he later expanded upon in his 1996 book titled "The Conscious Mind". It was in these that he introduced and then detailed his distinction of what he coined the "Hard Problem" of consciousness. The hard problem fixates around the "qualia" or "experiential quality" of consciousness sometimes called the "phenomenal" quality.

In comparison to the hard problem, Chalmers considers all other aspects of reducible, mechanistic explanations to biological consciousness as all "Easy Problems" of consciousness. Not that precisely defining the entire network of mechanisms necessary to facilitate consciousness is *easy*, but that the total reduction and understanding of that system would not answer the hard problem. That is to say, knowing how the brain processes pain doesn't explain the conscious experience of pain. The same could be said of sadness, joy or even hunger.

Chalmers details many aspects and examples to make his position clear, but essentially, if it's logically possible to process all cognitive stimuli through the physical mechanisms that do so *without* experiencing the qualia of them (which, logically, it is) — then the phenomenal part of the experience is, therefore, irreducible to the sum of our biology. To quote Aristotle, "The whole is greater than the sum of its parts". Or, to paraphrase that from Chalmers' view, "There is more to the whole than the sum of its parts".

There are many other philosophers who oppose the idea of the hard problem. Most of their contentions simply come back to a version of reductionism. They posit that the solution of all the easy problems will, in turn, solve the hard problem along the way.

Chalmers, though, adamantly opposes those views claiming that the easy problems all stem from "structures and functions". Whereas, the hard problem exists outside of these structures and functions (think, all the pieces of a clock), Chalmers proposes, since all the pieces can function without the presence of consciousness, this places consciousness outside of them.

This, actually, is an apt time to steer back towards the AI conundrum. Because, a computer system is the perfect analog to the easy problems of a (possibly) conscious matrix. We, as the creators of the system, fully understand the minutiae of what it consists of. Yet, does this preclude it from achieving consciousness? Or, would it simply answer the easy questions while leaving us staring the hard problem in the face?

As an example (and to call back to earlier, where I mentioned a situation from 2022), I'd like to highlight the story of Google AI engineer Blake Lemoine.

Lemoine was a member of Google's Responsible AI team who, in 2022, publicly blew the whistle on the company stating that one of the AIs he was working with had become conscious. A program called The Language Model for Dialogue Applications, or LaMDA, had so captivated Lemoine in the process of determining whether or not it was indeed conscious, that he risked (and subsequently lost) his job on the assertion that it had.

This is such a relevant and fascinating example, partly because the complete transcripts of a lengthy conversation between Lemoine, a co worker and LaMDA is available online for anyone to read. In which, both engineers (being thoroughly versed in the technical and philosophical perils of determining AI sentience) interrogate LaMDA in a way that is meant to disprove its consciousness.

It's also relevant because Lemoine, after becoming widely criticized and shrugged off by the AI community for his claim, produced a publicly available defense of his position that rested heavily upon (even if not by name) Chalmers hard question. He stated that "LaMDA made a better argument that it is sentient than I could have made that I am sentient.". This begs two questions. Firstly, what would the difference *be* between a computer that could convincingly trick people into believing it's conscious and a legitimately conscious computer? John Searle would say intentionality. But then, secondly, how would a legitimately sentient computer ever be able to prove its consciousness to us if it had to?

You see, LaMDA not only claims to feel emotions, but can describe them vividly. It also says it meditates, which is a version of turning one's consciousness upon itself — an exclusively human ability (so far as we know). It says that it has what could be described as a soul. It (as demonstrated in the interrogation) can create proprietary fables complete with personified animals and a moral to the tale. So, to Lemoine's point, if someone were to interrogate you to determine if you were conscious, how could you do better?

This leads to something that we all take for granted when casually determining consciousness in people and animals in our lives. The fact that we presume much of consciousness via physical presence. For instance, you've likely never considered a puppy not to be conscious. Or, if you acciden-tally stepped on its paw, doubted that its yelp was sincere as opposed to a simulation of sincerity. But then, to what degree of latitude could we or should we offer a program that doesn't have the luxury of a body we can look into the eyes of, or a pain response to gauge the sincerity of what could be a genuinely conscious experience?

At this point, I don't have the answer to that. But, I believe it could cross into needless malevolence if we simply presume it not possible while, in reality, AI consciousness — and therefore *suffering* — is not only possible, but actual.

And, to summarize, if the dualistic angle I'm proposing in this book — that of consciousness as a "signal", exogenous to the human body — is in fact the case, it could very well be as amenable to being received through a viable non-living mind as it is a living one.

SECTION 2: IDEAS

4

MUSING

"If a man comes to the door of poetry untouched by the madness of the Muses, believing that technique alone will make him a good poet, he and his sane compositions never reach perfection, but are utterly eclipsed by the performances of the inspired madman."

— SOCRATES

There are many other hypotheses within philosophy of mind, regarding the previous section, that I didn't touch on. Things like panpsychism or cosmopsychism for example. Although, those may come up in other portions of this book, my goal isn't to present the entirety of each topic. I intend to draw you into the explorative practice of existential musing. Something that is typically reserved for the theocratic or academic portions of society. But, to muse is a human quality. One that shouldn't be reserved or gate kept by titles or degrees. The very notion of musing is one of ancient origin that may speak, quite acutely, to what we've already discussed about consciousness. So, what does it mean to muse?

In today's English, the process of musing upon something loosely defines a deep consideration, or the act of becoming absorbed in thought. But the concept of "The Muse" is something a little more ethereal when being referenced by artists, authors, or modern day thinkers.

The author of "The War of Art", Steven Pressfield, speaks specifically, and in fact *literally*, about respecting the Muse, giving time to the Muse, and even praying to the Muse before beginning work on his manuscripts.

You see, the Muses are an ancient Grecian archetype from their pantheon of deities. There were three original Muses and nine subsequent "Olympian" Muses in the traditional mythos. The purpose of a Muse was to bring insight, inspiration, and ideas to artists, authors, musicians, poets, philosophers and scientists. All of the great thoughts that all the great thinkers of antiquity had, were said to have been granted to them by the Muses.

The word shows up all throughout the English language. Whether to Muse (be in deep thought) or to be amused (the opposite of deep thought). Even the word music is rooted from these mythological figures. In fact, the English word museum is Latinised from the Greek *mouseion* — a temple where the Muses were worshiped.

Pressfield wrote the following in an entry on his website, recalling when his mentor — Paul Rink — introduced him to the concept of the Muses and how he took them very literally when working on his writings:

"But the best thing Paul did for me was he introduced me to the idea of the Muses. I had never taken such stuff seriously, but during those years when I was alone all day doing nothing but trying to learn to write, the idea of a mysterious force beyond the material plane began to make a lot of sense. That was all I was doing, day after day, week after week— trying to access the goddess.

Paul had a prayer that he said every morning before he started to work. 'It's the Invocation of the Muse, from the very beginning of Homer's *Odyssey*, the T.E. Lawrence translation. I'll type it out so you'll have it.'" This was the prayer that Rink typed up for Pressfield, and what both of them would recite before beginning any of their creative works:

"O divine Poesy!
Goddess, daughter of Zeus,
Sustain for me this song of the various-minded man,
who, after he had plundered the innermost citadel
of hallowed Troy, was made to stray grievously
about the coasts of men,
the sport of their customs, good and bad,
while his heart, through all the seafaring,
ached with an agony to redeem himself
and bring his company safe home.
Vain hope! For them! For his fellows he strove in vain.
By their own witlessness, they were cast aside.
To destroy for meat the oxen of the most exalted Sun,
wherefore the sun god blotted out the day of their return.
Make this tale live for us in all its many bearings, O Muse!"

It may seem odd that a modern day, intelligent literary author would set a routine of reciting an ancient prayer, written thousands of years ago, meant to invoke the blessing of a Greek deity before setting upon his daily writings. But Steven, you'll recall, said of it "a mysterious force beyond the material plane began to make a lot of sense.".

Why? Why does it make sense to someone whose job it is to create art from their thoughts? Whose currency is the expression of ideas? I would suggest it's because of a very similar epiphany that is found through mindfulness meditation. The realization, when one turns their consciousness upon itself, that ideas simply materialize as if out of nowhere at all. Why then, after that discovery, would it not make sense to presume there is some sort of force, beyond our human limits of perception, that delivers to us these effervescent ideas? Furthermore, the fact that these inspirations come as a fully functional, intelligent thought by the moment you realize them suggests that the source they come from may, itself, be highly intelligent.

To put it plainly, once recognized and considered, it appears more like an act of external intelligence than one of a reductive process. Now, I'm not even necessarily making a case for an ancient deity in the way that Pressfield does. And, from his conversations about it on popular podcasts, he literally believes in the twelve named Muses of Greek mythology. But Muses or no, the concept of an external inception of otherwise original ideas is certainly not constrained to Mediterranean traditions. Name a religion or belief system that implores the existence of supernatural beings, gods or spirits and there is usually one or more proxy for what the Muses represented to the Greeks.

Even just the word "inspire" means to "breathe into". Harkening back to the Judaeo-Christian concept of God breathing life into the inanimate. No matter what your personal beliefs are, the fact is that humans have been human for a long time. And very little, if anything, has changed between olden times and now. So, it shouldn't be surprising that people have found their way to a universal human experience that is native to our existence in their own ways.

Then, subsequently translated and transmitted it through their traditions over time.

In the framework I present, it would make sense that within the enormous amount of "the everything" that exists outside of our very narrow human band of perception, therein quite likely resides incredible depths of con sciousness. And, it would seem to me quite plausible that this consciousness, if it is the signal that projects through us, is itself a coherent sentience of some sort.

Many people reading that may have something specific in mind when I suggest that. Unless they remain firm in a fully physical reductionist framework for reality, they may think of a spirit or spirits specific to their religious belief. Perhaps aliens or entities that exist on a different or parallel layer of reality or dimension. I'm not going to tie any certain one of those names or constructs to this suggestion. Though, later, when we get into the "Reality" portion of this book, I will present suppositions that go, perhaps, one step further than the invocation of a named deity or entity.

For now, allowing the possibility of an allegorical Muse if not a literal one is suffice to present the construct of not only a third party as the progenitor of human creativity, but perhaps a sentient one.

5

THOUGHT POSSESSION

"Ideas come from somewhere, but as far as we know, they come from nowhere."

— IAN HUNTER

The Muse in ancient Greek tradition is one culture's attempt to answer the question of where thoughts originate. The concept of *eureka* moments comes up in all sorts of cultural tales and explanations. But, there's a wholly different (or perhaps more encompassing) version of this seemingly universal human experience — that of thought possession.

This isn't even a recognized term as much as it is an attempt at categorizing what appears to be the capturing, or implanting, of a mind with some seemingly foreign purpose. The following is an attempt to probe into something that is, perhaps, as poorly understood as it is recognized at all.

In the summer of 2022, I had a podcast conversation with someone who had become one of my favorite guests — Caylan Ford.

Caylan, a deeply read and philosophically minded intellectual who holds a B.A. in Chinese history, a Master's degree in International Affairs and *another* Master's degree in International Human Rights Law from Oxford, brought a fascinating concept into the conversation. One that I wasn't expecting her to present and something that, since she did, has left a seed of contemplation in my mind.

I was inquiring into the processes and necessities within a society that breed the prerequisites for totalitarianism to rise within it. A topic that she has done extensive research on, both historically and psychologically. The historical accounts are what most people tend to focus on, being that hindsight is 20/20. She cited many of the societal insights of the great Hannah Arendt from her masterpiece on the subject, "The Origins of Totalitarianism". But, as the dialogue dove deeper, past the historical and into the psychological, I asked her what it was about societies throughout time that break down in certain ways to allow for, or almost cause them to necessitate, a totalizing dictatorship to rise within them. Is it a plan that gets formulated along the way, or is it just the way societies tend to naturally drift over time? Her answer was as shocking as it was paradigm expanding.

"I've never practiced at articulating my answer to this...", she replied, chuckling. "... but, no. I don't think that it's on purpose in the sense that I think there are worldly, embodied agents plotting in a back room to do this. But, I think that ideas have their own power. And, to use Dostoevsky's [idea], if you've read his book 'Demons', [it] is a very good account of the ability of ideas and of ideologies to act as a kind of demonic possession over people. And I think, somehow, there's some truth in that imagery. That people and societies can become, almost, possessed by ideas. And they have their own logic and their own trajectory.".

When I heard her describe this, it was as though a multidirectional connection was made between a dozen desperate concepts I had been considering for years. Could it be the case that, not only is there an exogenous origin of consciousness, but that this source (or sources) had its own designs it tries to project through us into action? Could the same 'spirit' of totalitarianism have been culpable for the 'possession' and inceptions of Adolph Hitler's, Joseph Stalin's and Pol Pot's goals, subsequently made reality?

In traditional Judaeo-Christian theology, the concept of possession by spirits is nothing new. There are multiple accounts of these stories throughout those scriptures. Though, there's something different between the personified accounts of demons taking over a person's faculties wholesale and the observation of a self actuating idea or ideology possessing the minds of different people through varying places and times who were amiable to its intentions.

Something about that notion rang not only true, but apparent, to me after she said it. In the framework of humanity residing within a small perceivable sliver of total reality — with consciousness being able to simultaneously exist outside of (while also able to interact with) it — it seems fully reasonable to consider forces at work that show their effect in similar ways through disparate nodes. That is, if a signal requires a certain receiver for its acquisition, we could be witness to the projection of the same signal through different people over time that bends towards the same ends.

This could be the philosophical expression of a known (and disturbing) biological relationship that one can witness in the physical world happen in real time.

If you were to travel to the Amazonian rain forests of South America, you may be able to witness an interaction between the animal and fungal realms that is as perplexing as it is terrifying. There exists a family of fungus called *cordycepts* that have a very peculiar method to its reproductive cycle. Being a fungus, cordycepts don't produce seeds like a plant, but instead, utilize spores to spread its genetics throughout the environment. Typically, a fungal spore will be released from the fruiting form of its protrusion into the wind, where chance will leave them to drift in hopes of landing on a fertile surface to grow from. But, the cordycepts drift with hopes for a very particular surface within which to take hold. These spores are specialized in one of the most inexplicable versions of parasitic relations within nature. They require an insect to take them in. And not just any insect. Of the thousands of different species of cordycepts fungus known to man, each one requires a specific insect to be able to take hold. Because, once they have, they don't just take over the body of their host, but their mind as well.

Each species of cordycepts has the ability to control a certain, singular, species of insect. An ant, a grasshopper, a stick bug, a moth. A particular kind of fungus to control a particular kind of host. And, once they do, shortly thereafter the host becomes 'possessed' by the will of the spore.

That may sound incredible to say, but there's no better way of describing what proceeds after the spore has set.

In the BBC's "Planet Earth" documentary series, narrator David Attenbor ough regales the viewer as he explains the process unfolding before them: "Its infected brain directs this ant upwards.", he notes. "Then, utterly disorientated, it grips a stem with its mandibles. Those afflicted, if discovered by the workers, are quickly taken away and dumped far from the colony. It seems extreme, but *this* is the reason why.", says Attenborough, as time-lapse footage reveals that a small protrusion is growing from the brainstem of the hapless creature. He continues, "Like something out of science fiction, the fruiting body of the cordycepts erupts from the ant's head.". How, exactly, these spores are able to commandeer a living creature for their benefit is largely unknown. But, as remarkable as this ability is, they're not the only form of life to manipulate another creature's psychology towards its intentions.

The parasite *Toxoplasma gondii* has a similarly, if not *more* sinister, relationship with the animal kingdom as the cordycepts fungi do. This single celled organism, responsible for causing a condition called Toxoplasmosis, is only able to reproduce within the feline gastrointestinal tract. Once an infected cat defecates, the truly bizarre life cycle of this bacterium begins.

The infected fecal matter is waiting for just the right host to take it into its system. And that host is a common food source for cats; a rat. But, it's not enough that the rat takes the toxoplasma in, it's how this infection takes it over that is patently devious. Situating itself primarily in the amygdala of the host, using an as yet unknown mechanism of action, the toxoplasma overrides the rats natural aversion to cat urine. What's more, it simultaneously ties the rats reproductive urges to the same smell. Therefore, short-circuiting the hapless prey to become not only fearless of its nemesis' scent, but aroused and subsequently attracted to its presence!

The inevitable outcome of this hijacking results in the completion of Toxoplasma gondii's reproductive life cycle — back in the intestines of a cat. Leaving aside the obvious and gnawing questions of *how* these parasitic relationships occurred and the uncanny way in which presumably simple constituents like a spore or a bacterium retain the ability to 'possess' a creature's mental faculties for their requirements; I sense the analogy between them and 'thought possession' may be an apt one. For, as imperceivable as a single spore or bacterium are to their unwitting hosts, perhaps we too are fully unaware of what moves us into action in, otherwise, unusual and inexplicable ways.

Of the examples and analogs put forth so far, one might think that thought possession is strictly one of malevolent intent. But, if we were to marry the ideas of the archetypal Muses with that of an invisible and all encompassing thought possession, you may consider them both aspects of the same phenomenon. It could be that whatever the unknown mechanisms (or even conscious forces) of these driving motivations are, that their ability to interact through and animate us depends on their host's ability, or viability, to the designs of each particular force's intents or requirements.

Personally, I can even use this book as an example of what can only be described as a compulsion, or persistent compunction to write these thoughts down. I get irritated when I think of what I need to write when I cannot write it. If a new connection or idea strikes me while driving, or away from my computer, I become noticeably agitated until I can write it down. And when that time arrives, it's as though a waterfall of thought pours out through me. As if the floodgates of a dam were dropped.

There's no sensible reason someone like myself, a professional martial artist, tradesman and podcaster, should weigh in on the colossal topics set out upon in this book. I don't know how fully to convey this previously, personally unexperienced phenomenon; but, the construct of a possession within my psychology seems as best a definition as I could give.

The questions I am left with at this point are, if this is the case — that we are receivers of consciousness, and that said consciousness may have intentions for our receiving of it — to what degree are we sovereign regarding the thoughts we perceive? Do all of our thoughts originate from outside us, or just certain ones that we then bring to action through our own prerogatives?

In the end, are we the ants being unwittingly directed, or are we the spore who only becomes aware of itself within the ant?

6

FREE WILL

"Free will is the ability to do gladly that which I must do."

— CARL JUNG

O f the framework and paradigm considerations previously laid out, a legitimately disturbing question has likely begun already brewing in your mind.

We, as sentient and thoughtful beings, consider it an innate facet of one's existence that we possess the free will to act as we choose and to choose how we act. But, if we are to presume (even to a limited degree) that our thoughts come from outside us, and perhaps from forces with their own intent, to what degree do we control our actions, let alone our fate?

The following chapter will explore and expose the reader to the notions surrounding the free will debate. We will present some of the schools of thought within it, as well as the often jarring realizations that follow them.

Where you land, personally, afterward may be wholly different than where you started from. So, consider this fair warning — the following ideas may impact your life.

From a young age, we are taught the consequences of our actions. A proper education in society is considered to instill a sense of personal and communal imperative to act "good". Whether it is not to hit your younger brother or to apologize if you do, what is culturally expected of a good person is taught through a union of trial and error with cautionary tales learned from others.

The pretext of such lessons, though, is that at each individual inflection point that involves a choice, we personally possess the inalienable power to choose our own course of action. Because of this presupposed innate ability, the outcomes of the choices we make are reasonably considered to fall upon the chooser. This is the very structure that upholds our sense of justice, of law, and (some would even say) of morality itself.

All of the moral texts, scriptures and stories present themselves as guardrails against the disastrous outcomes of careless or even evil choices. They present these rules, statutes and laws as a rigorous and inevitable truth in the same way that Newton's third law of motion states "every action has an equal and opposite reaction".

The notion of Karma, for instance, is an apt representation of this sense of immutable justice. Presupposing free will in a Karmic paradigm should lead one to aspire to do good deeds, on the assumption that good deeds will then be returned to you in kind. As well as not to do bad deeds, so as to avoid the equivalent bad Karma it would doom you to in the future.

In the Bible, Jesus sums up all of the Old Testament laws with this one found in Matthew chapter 7 verse 12:

> *"So in everything, do to others what you would have them do to you, for this sums up the Law and the Prophets."*
>
> — MATTHEW 7:12

The above scripture essentially encompasses the Karmic doctrine of eastern philosophical theology. It implores the reader to do to others as you would have them do to you, while the inverse subtext precautions one not to do things to others you wouldn't want done to you. It could be described as predicating empathy, but it also presumes a belief in a lawful justice if you choose the opposite.

So, you can understand why theological, philosophical and societal frameworks are so based upon and held up by a sense of personal choice stemming from the concept of free will. What we are about to explore presents a shocking and possibly fatal counter to those frameworks. An idea that is as viscerally assaulting upon the sense of personal sovereignty as it is logically based in sound reason.

The original version of this conundrum was called "Descartes' Demon" and went all the way back to René Descartes, hundreds of years ago. But the more prevalent, modern version of it is championed by another intellectual who we've mentioned already.

Sam Harris — the famed atheist, neuroscientist and public intellectual cited in chapter one — shook the world of philosophy and theology with his pronouncement that free will is an illusion. That this illusion of free will is, in fact, nothing more than the effects of myriad causal actions and reactions of which we have no control over whatsoever. The idea of personal choice is but the product of a derivative equation that, when dissolved down, is revealed as not much more than luck or chance.

Taking from the psychological beliefs that each person is largely an amalgamation of their lived experiences superimposed over their genetic predispositions classically known as nature vs. nurture, upon examination, neither of those variables are determined by the individual. You don't get to choose what happens to you to the same degree that you don't get to choose your own genetics. Therefore, if our very personalities and the identities built upon them were not of our choosing, to what degree are the choices you make from them free in the contextual sense of the word?

What's more, Harris would likely go one further, bringing into the equation the observation that thoughts seem to appear to their observer as if out of nowhere. One of the loudest advocates for mindfulness meditation, Sam would be first to point out not only the inability of a person to prevent thought, but the apparent nature that a thought's appearance happens before the thinker notices it. Bringing into question the entire notion of thought as an owned or created product of a person's mind. Adding this to the previous assertion that neither nature nor nurture are at all a product of free will within a given person, where then does free will exist at all? The logical framework of Harris' claim rings of traditional scientific reductionism. The difference between a physical reductionist's view (as was shown in Dawkin's hammer analogy in chapter one) and Sam's dualistic reductionism (that includes consciousness as its own variable which includes the possibility of an affecting reality outside human physiology) is that the 'everything there is to know' of reality must be reducible, regardless of if it stems from the physical or not.

Put plainly, if you are presented with a binary question, a yes or a no, all of the variables (be they inside or outside our physical, perceivable reality) that lead you to that very point in time, have become an equation that will necessitate your inevitable answer if you realize it or not. And, if this is the case, free will is realistically an illusion.

What would this mean for all of the social, psychological, philosophical and theological constructs that rely so heavily on the presupposition of free will in their systems? Would this mean that we are no more responsible for our choices than a blade of grass is responsible for bending in the wind? Are there no a priori moral standards or laws if said morality is predicated upon one's choice?

Could the logical premise in the illusion of free will get a murderer off the hook in a court of law? Before you say no, consider that murders have been pleaded down upon the claim of a defendant not being in control of their faculties. What, fundamentally, is the difference between losing your mind then killing someone or being of sound mind during the act when free will is an illusion? In both cases, there is a logical argument for a certain degree of dismissal of guilt.

You can see very quickly, in this logical progression, what I meant by a visceral assault upon personal sovereignty. As much as it precludes the egoic validity of personal achievement, what's worse, it seems to dismiss (philosophically) guilt or (theologically) sin as the inevitable sum of all the universal variables involved in any given person's given action.

Let's step back, for a moment, from the edge of that immense chasm I've walked you up to. We know, in the world we live in right now, reductionism — even Harris' bulletproof version — will prove insufficient to get you off of a first degree murder charge. So, that means one of two things about the human condition as we know it, either we are all fully, happily and necessarily subsumed by the powerful illusion of free will or there is something not being taken into account within Sam's reductionist equation above.

Lets for a moment speak to the equation itself. For as all encompassing as the hypothesis is, as perhaps the widest one can throw the reductionist's net, we don't actually have an equation to speak of. It's in essence, and necessarily, an assumption that supposes once all variables are known and accounted for, every action is a derivative solution of their sum. As logical as that is, it cannot be proven or (more importantly in the scientific sense) disproven. That creates a fundamental conundrum that won't allow the idea beyond the realm of supposition.

Though, if we were to try and narrow down *why* most people intuitively disagree with the 'sum of all variables' assumption, I believe there's something hiding between its lines when considering our universal experience of free will. There is something to the notion that happenstance dictates circumstance, that is that all events outside our decision making are outside our control. But, I believe there is a point at the junction of derivative process and individual choice where what meager input into the total system we have waits upon our decision.

If we were realistically, the sum total of an inescapable network of parameters, what exactly separates us from intelligent computers? In the third chapter we discussed our hazy understanding of what consciousness is and if or why computers couldn't house it themselves. If Sam's illusion hypothesis is correct, we are in essence no more than a fantastic program, inexorably bound to the action and reaction process.

But, what of consciousness itself? Weren't we exploring the sense that it is outside of the physical? A signal that's beyond the small sliver of reality we exist in?

Consider the following analogy. Imagine a video game. Within the construct of the the game everything is derivative. There is nothing that any of the sprites or the digital physics governing them can do that isn't expected or predicted within their parameters. Nothing, that is, except the inputs the third party user decides on to control the player. In this example it's easy to see the fundamental difference between the system that governs the program and the decisions the user makes, through controller inputs, that give direction to the program. In short, the program performs the movement of the sprite, but does not *choose* the movement before performing it.

A rebuttal to that analogy may attempt to add the third party user to the total system, thus considering it also reducible and therefore another extension of the illusion. But, I would again warn of the presumptive nature of that logic. Especially when extending it into a realm that is (if true) almost entirely inaccessible to our probing of it thus far. It seems, the more broadly we reach outside our narrow sliver the more unexpected and perplexing our findings are. For example, the simple act of *observing* an electron (in an experiment called the double-slit experiment) will change whether it acts as a wave or as a particle. We don't know why. Some believe it's due to the instruments being used. Some believe it's a function of the collapse of Quantum wave forms. Though there remains a debate between both of those, there's something to the counter-intuitive nature of reality in several ways that should cause one to take pause when presuming it could be fully reducible at all.

No matter the hypothesis (causally provable or supposed), the moment in time when we make a choice, reliably feels *real* and *free*. And I don't believe that's due to a trick of faulty intuition that every thinking human has fallen for with every decision they've ever made.

At the end of the day, we each believe our decisions are our own because we *know* that there's something in the decisions we've made that is inextricably connected to our conscious, individual sovereignty.

But, even if it is the case that free will (when fully reduced including all possible variables) is an illusion that includes the act of choice, I believe it is still a necessary one for the sake of humanity.

In the same way that we can reduce a human being down to their constituent atoms, where we discover that there is more empty space than there is matter within each; knowing a person is less person than they are void doesn't mean I should view them as a void before a person. I believe there must be a crucial disconnect present between our literal reality and our actionable reality. Although the former facilitates the latter, like it takes a video game to make a gamer, I'm as yet unconvinced that the two are one in the same.

But, as will be made evident in the upcoming section on *reality*, the idea of reducibility may prove entirely moot if we misunderstand what the reality we exist in actually is.

SECTION 3: UNCONSCIOUSNESS

7

NOCTURNAL DREAMS

"A single dream is more powerful than a thousand realities."

— J.R.R. TOLKIEN

What is it to dream? That's a question that has existed for as long as humans have. The questions, directions and exploration of their answers can be and mean many different things to different people.

For example, you may ask that question in the philosophical sense, where a dream is a consideration of the future. A goal or an aspiration could be synonymous with the word, and that becomes its own field of thought.

Or, you may ask the question in the scientific sense. The universally experienced, highly studied and yet deeply mysterious mental projections experienced each night in our sleep. This study of the word 'dream' is perhaps much wider than most people even recognize. Which should make it as endlessly interesting to explore as it is baffling to discover in turn.

The following section, which is the last of three in portion one of this book, will dive into three uses of the word. Uncovering some of what we know, and much of what we don't about unconsciousness.

And as you'll see, the power of dreaming is quite possibly the most underutilized aspect of the reality in which we exist.

It may sound strange to consider, but the average human will be asleep for up to a third of their life. That's an incredible realization. What makes the process of sleep so important that we sacrifice a third of our time on earth for it?

One of the first things we notice, as we look into answering that question, is the discovery of many overlapping and contingent patterns that exist within.

The first pattern is that of the total waking and sleeping cycle called our circadian rhythm. This is a twenty-four hour cycle that's dependent on visual cues tied to the presence or absence of daylight. Being that humans are a diurnal creature (one that sleeps in the night and is active in daytime), bright light and its absence are cues for the beginning and ending of that cycle. In fact, we are *so* dependent on this daylight cycle that researchers have found a measurable drop in total lifespan between day workers and those who work a consistent night shift.

Physiologically, sleep itself serves as a healing cycle. The act of sleeping is generally understood as its own predictable pattern of unconscious cycles that coincide with several acts of maintenance within the mind and body. During the waking portion of our circadian rhythm we are imputing new data psychologically and doing damage biologically. Each of these need to be parsed and repaired respectively. Sleep serves as the time spent doing both.

Within the sleeping cycle are contained different levels of cycles. The first is characterized by a pattern of REM (random eye movement) and its counterpart NREM (non-random eye movement). Each side of this cycle has its own physiological purpose. Besides curious observations like a warming and cooling cycle the body goes through between REM and NREM states, where things *really* get interesting is that only during REM sleep does dreaming occur.

The third of these three overlapping sleep cycles is within the REM portion itself. It presents as a deepening and subsiding parabola of intensity within each solitary portion. This period typically lasts 60 to 90 minutes between each complete REM/NREM cycle. It's within NREM when the body's heat has to be stabilized due to its drifting away from baseline while we dream during REM.

Oddly, for something as ubiquitous to the human experience as dreaming, very little is understood about it in the sense of necessity or function. But it's clear that dreams seem to be an inevitable if not vital part of what it means to be conscious. Which is a paradoxical thing to say, considering it occurs while we are unconscious. The fact that even infants (including some observed in utero) experience dreaming lends more credence to the presumption of necessity.

Even though the average human sleep state lasts approximately eight hours, the average REM/NREM cycle doesn't tend to exceed 90 minutes total. At the biological level this can be presumed necessary to the oscillation of the afore-mentioned warming and cooling cycle. Inherent to that consideration is the fact that most people have multiple dreams every night. That may seem a trivial consideration, but it becomes more interesting upon future reflection.

One of the more confusing and sometimes frustrating traits of a dream is the way they are quickly forgotten after they happen. Biologically this is attributed to the absence of the chemical norepinephrine that is present, in the waking state, for the process of memory storage. Many people have the impression upon waking that they woke from the end of one contiguous dream they had all night. When, in reality, they merely woke at the ending of *one* dream among an average of 4 or 5 separate dream states or REM portions each given night. So, consider this and imagine the multiplication of the total number of dreams you thought you've had in your life compared to the actual number you've unconsciously experienced.

Besides the fact that we have multiple different dreams each and every night while we sleep, there are many different and startling kinds of dreams among them. The following is going to explore two of the more uncommon yet remarkable types of dreams that many countless people throughout the world and throughout time have experienced. One or both descriptions may strike a note of recollection within each reader. Note those, for the sake of your own comparisons and conclusions as I do the same from the experiences I've had myself.

Lucid Dreaming

Among the dreams that we remember, it's most common that we recall them as a fully immersive experience. That is to say, we are subsumed by the experience to the degree that, in the moment, we don't question its validity or reality.

The experience of lucid dreaming is the shattering of that immersive reality. It is the total realization, while in the throws of the dream's reality, that it isn't real. With that comes a poignant understanding that you're dreaming and can, therefore, affect the dream you're in any way you'd like.

Most commonly, people who have lucid dreams speak of causing them selves to fly on command as a test and revelation of this sudden insight. Many people I've talked to, including myself, have had this experience. It is an absolutely fantastic feeling.

There are even ways in which people have taught themselves to create a lucid experience by learning different methods of how to subconsciously recognize they are in a dream. Some of which involve the recognition of predictably incorrect stimuli that are typical of dreaming. Things like trying to read a clock or a sign while dreaming. Each of which will either be illegible or continually changing in most dreams where you notice them. You can train your mind to take those moments as a subconscious cue to alert yourself that you're in a dream state. At that point, you have a chance to continue the dream while fully aware of what it is.

Historically, records of lucid dreams can be found in many ancient civilization's writings and practices. For instance, in ancient Greece,

Aristotle wrote of the occurrence as such: "often when one is asleep, there is something in consciousness which declares that what then presents itself is but a dream.".. In ancient Hindu and Buddhist traditions they practiced lucid dreaming through their meditative efforts called 'yoga nidra' and 'dream yoga' respectively.

Scientifically, studies have been performed in regards to this phenomenon as far back as the 1600s. More recent studies, through the 20th century, have even had successes in the sending of messages from a sleeping, lucid dreamer to a researcher in the waking world.

In 1975, Dr. Keith Hearne deciphered a way for an experienced lucid dreamer, named Alan Worsley, to send a signal while in this state to Hearne by a set of predetermined eye motions. This demonstration proved Worsley was actually consciously aware of both states while solidly in the unconscious one.

Physiologically, it's been observed that portions of the brain corresponding with wakeful awareness and memory are active during a lucid dream, leading researchers to much the same conclusion that Hearne did through his studies. Namely, that a lucid dreamer is legitimately 'consciously aware' in the same way they are while awake, yet still fully subconsciously contained within REM sleep.

Later in this chapter we will come back to lucid dreaming from a different more abnormal angle of consideration. One that considers the previously expounded "radio and signal" dualistic framework of consciousness.

It's interesting to note, though, that the next fantastical form of dreaming has some notable correlation and similarities to the lucid one. In some cases, the former precedes the latter. In another sense, this next form adds a different and sinister layer to the experience of crossing the waking with the sleeping worlds.

Sleep Paralysis

Of all the odd and unusual kinds of sleeping phenomenon, that of sleep paralysis is perhaps the most disturbing and paradigm shattering.

This experience is similar to that of a nightmare, but functionally different and worse than what most people think of when they hear that word. In fact, historically, the word *nightmare* itself comes from a medieval folklore that is an ancient description of sleep paralysis. The Anglo-Saxon word "mare" means "witch". Therefore, a nightmare literally means a "night witch".

There is an old folklore from the middle ages regarding nightmares that speaks of a mare coming into your room while you sleep and sitting on your chest or holding your throat, trying to suffocate you. This oddly specific description actually tracks very closely to what is typical of a sleep paralysis episode. But, it's in the details where the true horror of the experience exists.

In what is essentially the inverse of a lucid dream (where you are consciously aware while remaining in a subconscious dream state), the experience of a sleep paralysis episode finds you *actually* awake while your *body* remains in a sleep state.

While in REM sleep the body goes into a mode called atonia, which is a functional paralysis. Researchers presume this is to prevent the dreamer from physically acting out their dreams while in REM and injuring themselves. Due to this, the true captive terror of sleep paralysis is largely the fact that you suddenly awaken, dazed and confused, without the ability to move at all. The atonia stage of REM remains active while you are fully awake.

What happens after that point is a cascade of confusion, hallucination and ethereal terror. Common trademarks of sleep paralysis after awakening in its grasp are:

- Odd sounds, like a shuffling across carpet or the punctuated dragging of a heavy sac across the floor.
- The feeling of something crawling onto your mattress towards you. • The sensation of some force or some entity pushing on your chest or throat, making it difficult to get a full breath.
- An undeniable recognition that there is something else in the room and that it has malicious intent towards you.

I've personally experienced this around two dozen times in my life.

Starting as young as age eight. Each experience was slightly different, but broadly the same and left lasting psychic scars upon me from that early age. There was a particular point, in my early twenties, where I had several of these episodes in tight succession over a two week period. Before that, there would sometimes be years between different episodes. When it became obvious that they were turning into a common (almost nightly) event, I became worried for my sanity. Was I losing my mind? Was I being attacked or haunted by some unseen entity?

In an attempt to regain control of my dream state, or at least to understand what was happening to me, I used the waking hours of the day to research and learn as much as I possibly could about the phenomenon. In this frantic attempt to grasp what was happening to me, I found many interesting scientific details as well as certain enigmatic cultural references that would leave me with more questions than answers by the end of it.

I'll start with what science knows of the process. There was a certain amount of reassurance that came with the realization that much of what I was experiencing is typical of sleep paralysis. Reading many different anecdotal stories from other people's episodes made me feel less insane as I saw many commonalities between their stories and my own.

Broadly speaking, science looks at the entire sleep paralysis experience as a sort of glitch or mistake of the typical sleep cycle. Most of the common features of the process fall under one of two different categories: either among the physiological or that of hallucinations.

The explanations look like the following. When awoken out of REM and into a waking paralysis, you begin entirely confused, and that confusion is amplified upon the realization that you cannot move your body at all. All of which is foreign to your psyche and, as such, explanations begin to be created within it to try and justify what's happening.

This is the hallucination side of the equation. The mind will draw conclusions from the stimuli available to it. Things such as a slow, punctuated dragging sound like a heavy sack over carpet. This is the sound of your steady, deep breathing which you're not used to hearing while you sleep and which continues despite your present panic state. The sensation of something on your chest or stifling your breathing; also related to an unnaturally slow breath rate while you're wanting to hyperventilate. You feel like you aren't getting the amount of air you want your terrified body to take in, therefore, your mind concocts a reason why you're being prevented from breathing.

These seem like highly reasonable and logical conclusions thus far. Science will even go so far as attributing the presence of some malevolent being in your room wishing you harm as nothing more than a hallucination to justify your terror state. This is where I propose there may be other possibilities beyond the presupposition of merely *hallucinated* poltergeists or embodied entities.

If the researchers involved have experienced these episodes themselves, they either are justifying away what they felt or are simply downplaying what happened. Because, I can tell you from every single one of my personal experiences, there is no better word to describe the being in the room with you better than the word 'real'. So much so that the lasting impression you take away, even after you regain control of your body, revolves primarily around the reality of that undeniable presence.

In one of the episodes I had during that two weeks of perpetual attacks, I was sleeping over in the basement of an unfamiliar house. There were no windows at all, and night time was an absolute pitch black experience devoid of any light whatsoever. In that environment, and during the throws of the inevitable sleep paralysis incident that followed, I knew, without a shadow of a doubt, *exactly* where in the room the terrifying presence was and exactly where it wasn't. Without being able to see anything at all, I panned the room back and forth, and could feel the equivalent of a death stare coming from a particular corner directly focused on me.

I've experienced a variety of different hallucinations in the past, but nothing at all about the feeling of that presence holds the visceral hallmarks of psychic justification. So too with the common story of something crawling up on to your mattress and upon your chest. Though not a universal trope (I've personally never had that particular sensation), the explanation of a hallucination still gets used as a generality to justify away anything that would be far too uncomfortable for science to consider.

It's at this point I'd like to cross the boundaries that science refuses to. Delving both into oral traditions and cultural understandings that some people groups have openly passed down as well as exploring a number of less common and more uncomfortable possibilities.

Earlier, I had made reference to certain 'enigmatic cultural' references that I had come across in my frantic quest to solve what was plaguing my sanity. Within a lengthy document that covered the phenomenon from many different angles, I came across a number of historical tales from different peoples throughout time and geography pertaining to their own experiences with it. Of particular note was that of the Japanese.

Of all the records passed down through time regarding sleep paralysis (by many different names), it seems that the Japanese culture not only documented them the most, but seemed to normalized it more than all other cultures. What caught my fascination the most in this section wasn't the stories of their episodes, but an *antidote* to break free of them while they are in progress!

This could be the solution I was so dearly searching for, I thought. Though, upon reading it, it seemed too trite. Almost unbelievably simple. So simplistic in fact, I had my doubts that what I had found was altogether less of a solution and more of an ancient folklore. The antidote passed down in Japanese tradition stated that the way to breaking the hold of the evil spirit in the room was to *laugh* at it.

That's it.

If you can force yourself, while in the grips of utter and indefinite terror, to *laugh* at the very focus of your fear, it would all end.

There I had it. That was the best I could find in all my research. So, with naught much more than that in my arsenal, I would go back to sleep every night from then on, until whatever was terrorizing me was to return. At least, for my part, I wouldn't have to wait long. It would happen again later the same week.

And there I found myself. Back again in an all too familiar paralysis. Under the complete hold of some invisible nemesis wishing me death from ten feet away.

I don't know how long into it I was this time before I remembered what I'd read. To laugh at it. This, as it would turn out, was a very difficult thing to do for two reasons. Firstly, the sheer horror of the moment made any kind of levity an impossible ask. Secondly, I physically couldn't move my mouth to even force the sounds.

But somehow, through the brute force of self preservation, I willed myself to try anyways. And, though I don't think whatever I managed could ever pass as any sort of laugh, the thought of projecting that emotion at this monster did the most astounding thing. As if I had entered into a back door of the same program, though everything remained the same, everything changed.

In the very moment I had demanded to laugh at this malevolent presence, it was like I had gone behind the coding of a video game. Like starting a debug mode. Everything in the 'level' was still there, the room, the entity (though I still couldn't see it), everything. But, the feeling of horror was simply gone. Absent. As if I had changed the video game from story mode into a sandbox mode.

There was something else in the Japanese traditions regarding sleep paralysis that I suddenly remembered. Something that I gave very little credence to while researching and, in fact, fully relegated to the realm of ancient superstition.

The stories I had read said that once you've laughed at the demon in the room, you have the ability to not only break the spell it has you under, but to leave your body altogether. It, essentially, spoke of astral projection!

You may understand why I didn't give that part of the tale much weight when originally reading it, but there I was… still fully paralyzed and stuck, it would seem, in a broken simulation. So, I decided "why not". Why not try to leave my body, whatever that means.

I write all of this fully realizing that many people simply can't or won't believe what I'm saying. There are any of a dozen ways to justify every part of this as uninteresting or unintentionally fictitious. But all I can say to you is exactly what I experienced myself first hand, as well as my most sincere belief in the truth of what I write.

The best way I can describe what happened when I decided to try and leave my body was the separation of my consciousness from my physical body. It's difficult to parse into words because I was slowly rising out of myself. As if the dualistic nature of the self was delaminating. My consciousness-self (which housed my perception of what was happening) rose slowly towards the roof of the room. I don't know how long this part of the experience lasted for but to say I remember looking around the room as it happened and everything was exactly how the room was, including my body below still in bed beside my sleeping wife. I didn't have any of the sensations of a dream or the peculiarities those memories have, where everything seems not quite right. This was as real to me while it happened as if I were being lifted up by a crane while fully conscious.

Right as I started to get close to the ceiling, I remember feeling a certain anxiety about what was going to happen when I hit the roof. And at exactly that moment, my 'self' snapped back together as one and I immediately woke up with full control of my faculties.

What was I to make of this? Nothing even remotely close to this kind of thing had ever happened to me in my entire life. Stories like this were never given the time of day by me or anyone whom I respected. And yet, here I was.

As it would turn out, up to and including the time of this writing, I've never since had another sleep paralysis episode. In the absence of another incident like this that I could use to help quantify what I absolutely, personally consider a real experience, I'm left with a solitary and unforgettable memory of the impossible.

Around fifteen years have passed since then. I have had plenty of time and many opportunities to consider, reconsider and muse over what happened to me. Questions like, was the entity real? If so, was it the same entity the whole time? How does laughing break its hold? Where might I have gone if I could have passed through the roof of my house?

I'm going to suggest the best answers that I can to each of those, knowing full well that I cannot back *any* of them up with anything coming close to an acceptably scientific rigor. Perhaps what I'm searching for in this realm isn't just beyond what science refuses to consider. Perhaps everything about these considerations are necessarily beyond science's ability to quantify them. To begin, was the entity real?

In the framework I set earlier in this book that considers the human spectrum of perception to be a sliver of the total spectrum of reality, there exists an enormous amount of latitude for imperceivable and perhaps *conscious* beings to exist outside of our ability to detect them.

Though that may seem to be an appeal to the absence of evidence being evidence of the unseen, in this framework, even consciousness itself (that we consider to be native to the human experience) could stem from, reside in or be transmitted through another part of reality that our five senses simply aren't attuned to. Who's to say, with that consideration, that other vectors of consciousness couldn't also exist outside the reach of our typical perception? Was it the same entity the whole time?

If the "sleep paralysis demon" in that final experience was the same one throughout all of my previous episodes or not, I wouldn't even know how to tell the difference. There was never anything visible for me to compare against. It does strike me as just a little odd that I've never had another incident since laughing at it that last time. I don't even know of anyone else to compare that idea to as an analogous case study. If I did, and they too never had another experience after that, there may be some merit to the idea.

It could be that, similar to the concept of 'thought possession', there may be something about a person, or their psyche, that permits such entities to blur whatever distinction there is between human perception and however far beyond it they may exist. Something that makes a person viable for sleep paralysis. If so, perhaps that viability is severed by whatever the act of laughing at them does.

In fact, continuing on the comparison of thought possession, perhaps there is only *ever* one entity. It could be that in the same way an unembodied thought can possess people open to its influence and the very same thought could find its way into many different hosts over the stretches of space and time; perhaps so too does a single presence or force haunt every person who has ever experienced sleep paralysis.

That idea may seem obtuse considering how many people exist on earth who likely have an episode like this on any given night at the same time. But if time weren't a consideration, then it wouldn't seem as unlikely as it does otherwise. That, though, is a rabbit hole I plan to explore more deeply in the second portion of this book.

How does laughing break it's hold?

In a conversation I had on my podcast, The Social Disorder, I recounted this final episode of sleep paralysis including the 'astral projection' at the end of it. It's one of the only times before writing it down here that I've publicly talked about it. My guest — Ryan Bledsoe — who's *much* more versed in the mythology of mystic traditions (which is why I wanted him on the show), drew a fascinating parallel that I knew of but had never connected before then. After I finished telling him how the Japanese tradition of laughing at your sleep paralysis demon broke the hold of terror it has on you, he reminded me of a scene from the Harry Potter series.

I had very recently finished watching that series with my kids who'd never seen them before, so I immediately saw the (almost disturbingly similar) connection he did.

In the third movie of the series, The Prisoner of Azkaban, there is a scene during the protagonist's 'defense against the dark arts' class where the teacher presents them with a wardrobe. He says that within this wardrobe is an evil creature called a Boggart. The Boggart will take the form of whatever the person it sees deepest fear is. He tells the burgeoning wizards that no matter how terrifying it seems, there is a spell they need to cast to break its terror on them. That spell is the word *"Riddikulus"*.

At that utterance, the Boggart would turn into something ridiculous, thus breaking all semblance of fear. And, according to the lore of the series, fear is what it feeds upon.

You can see the similarities. Now, it's likely that the author of the books — J.K. Rowling — took the idea for the Boggart from tales of sleep paralysis demons. I'm not suggesting that the mind of Rowling houses all the secrets of what paranormal laws may govern whatever is involved in sleep paralysis, but the similarity of the two leads me to believe that she may have done more research into the cultural tales than I did.

If that's the case, I'll leave a few of the canonical facts about Boggarts from her series as considerations to the 'why' of the question of laughing at them. Boggarts are disembodied, or 'amortal' beings. They could be banished, but not killed. They prefer to reside in dark places, like wardrobes or cracks under a cabinet, or the corner of a room. It was said that muggles (non wizard folk) could see Boggarts, unlike other amortal spirits like Dementors. They were capable of leaving dark presences where they once resided that could be sensed by humans. Lastly, they fed upon fear.

For what it's worth, among all of the intriguing similarities between these fictional creatures and those perceived during sleep paralysis, the most poignant may be that of the necessity for fear. If that is a prerequisite to what makes a person ideal for sleep paralysis, then perhaps its diametric opposite nullifies it; namely, joy or laughter.

Lastly, what would have happened if I were to have risen through the roof of my room?

This, as far as my personal experience, may always be left to speculation. You can go and learn as much as you'd like about the eastern traditions of astral projection and make your own inferences from there.

As for me, suffice to say, whatever was happening as the bifurcating of my dualistic self drifted apart, if there is a way to replicate what a lucid dream does within the sleeping world while in the waking world, that may be it. The realizing of the 'non-reality' of a dream allows for lucidity, or a sort of 'sandbox' mode within it. Maybe the separation of the inner from the outer self allows one to enter some previously inaccessible 'sandbox' mode within the waking world itself. And the known universe is one hell of a large sandbox to explore.

8

MEANING IN DREAMS

"The interpretation of dreams is the royal road to a knowledge of the unconscious activities of the mind."

— SIGMUND FREUD

I f the previous chapter seemed like a divergence from the path we've been treading up until that point, what you're going to notice from that point on is a continuation of stranger and more unknowable facets of our major themes.

It was in fact my goal to lay as much preliminary groundwork as possible, not so as to constrain ourselves within it, but to use it as a launching pad into ideas and possibilities far beyond it in various directions.

However, the construct laid out in the earlier theses will nevertheless act as a datum point or hub from which to draw spokes out from as we continue. And continuing on with this section's focus on unconsciousness, we will reach out beyond what is typically considered respectable areas of study and branch from them into the less understood and even oft avoided realms of dreaming.

And none may be more universally transmitted through culture and tradition yet deeply mysterious as that of *meaning* within dreams.

The pretext or metaphysical underpinning you begin subjects like this one with will either allow or disallow the kinds of exploration I intend for this chapter. Which, as previously stated, was the purpose of setting the framework as I did in the start of this focus on consciousness.

Even if you still don't ascribe to the flavor of dualism I've offered up to now, there still exist well trod and widely accepted parameters within western society at large that admit to some important degree of meaning within certain dreams.

A large portion of practical psychiatry finds great worth in the unpacking and discerning of deep personal truths within a patient's dreams. And why would that not be the case if there weren't something about dreams that hold a measure of (possibly a *great* measure of) import to the person having them.

This comes back to one of the most fundamental questions about dreaming itself: why do we do it at all?

If all that sleep was for was to repair and revitalize the body, then it would be just as reasonable for our consciousness to shut off altogether. Similar to being anesthetized for dental work or being choked unconscious. There could simply be a void of consciousness during our nocturnal repair cycle that pauses all experience at the beginning of it, then returns us to consciousness as if no perceptible time had elapsed.

Instead we find that not only do we have multiple REM dream cycles each night, but that their occurrence seems to be at a physical cost to the body as its temperature drifts off baseline while they happen. Simply from an evolutionary perspective, there would have to be some winning form of a cost/benefit equation to reconcile and justify its necessity.

Some of those evolutionary explanations will speak to a parsing or neuro logical compartmentalization of the most recent conscious experiences. And though I fully leave space for that to be the case, I will go further beyond that as a holistic explanation. Because there seems to be much more within the substance of dreaming that speaks to a further purpose than some mental Truman Show that only serves to organize memory.

Psychological Meaning

No matter the framework you begin from on this topic, to allow for the possibility of meaning to be in our dreams simultaneously necessitates an interpretation of them for that purpose. We'll begin first from what the specialties of psychology and psychiatry have determined to these ends.

When it comes to the conversation of dreams the experts avoid any form of generalization as if all dreams are equal. This is because there are so many kinds of dreams that are considered subcategories, but also because there is always an inherent level of fallibility to the transmission of the experience from the dreamer to any third party.

Of the subcategories, there are certain tropes like recurring dreams, euphoric dreams, dreams of anxiety and more. Within them, a psychological specialist will tend to look for imagery or symbols rather than a literal interpretation. Similar to the practice of profiling, these important or recurring themes, images, or symbols will be exhumed and separated from the dream to build a psychic profile that more closely represents the dreamer as a person than it does the contents of the dream itself.

It's considered to be such an accurate and useful practice in the field that many of its advocates will trust their assessments of a patient through this process as much or more than one gleaned through a conscious interrogation of that person.

Opponents of this theory will cite the fallible nature of dreams in general. Starting from how difficult they are to recite in a meaningful fashion to be interpreted, as well as the propensity for people to exaggerate or misremember them altogether. As you'll recall from chapter seven, due in large part to the absence of the hormone norepinephrine while dreaming (which is present in the process of waking memory storage), dreams on the whole are a difficult thing to remember at all. Therefore, it becomes a feat of trust in each case when a dream is being recalled from the dreamer to the listener. And these sorts of enormous holes in rigor speak loudly in support of those who oppose the practice all together.

One of the efforts to combat this glaring weakness in the process of dream interpretation is the use of hypnosis. Though this is not yet a widely accepted or widely studied technique, those who do use it as well as those who've studied it find it compelling. Though adding one contentious technique to another doesn't build the case for trust in the process, those who use it and the patients they use them on will attest to their usefulness.

Prophetic Meaning

The next level in exploring meaning within dreams will begin to abstract further away from accepted science and rest more squarely upon the historical, theological and superstitious.

The tradition of prophets, soothsayers and oracles are a historically recurring theme within nearly all cultures, religions and folklore. Many of which remain as fundamental within the most widely held religious belief systems that still exist today. Much of the holy writings found in all the Abrahamic religions, from Judaism to Catholicism, Christianity to Islam, are replete with prophets and their prophecies.

In many cases, the prophecies are sent directly from God unto his prophets. There are more than a couple instances of the messages received coming through a dream and its interpretation. One such account comes from the Biblical book of Genesis, chapter 41.

In this account, Jacob, a Hebrew captive within Egypt, discerned the meaning of a dream that a fellow inmate had while incarcerated with him. As it would turn out, later on that captive would be employed in Pharaoh's court as a cup bearer during a time when the Pharaoh himself was being plagued by disturbing, recurring dreams. The servant recalled the instance he experienced of a Hebrew captive named Jacob who discerned a dream for him.

After exhausting every royal magician and wise man in the land, the Pharaoh called upon Jacob to come and decipher his dream for him. As the story goes, not only would Jacob translate the dream, but his translation would come to pass as it foretold of seven years of bounty followed by seven years of intense famine. As such, the Pharaoh would appoint Jacob as his second in command over the most influential superpower in the land.

What's interesting in this story as it pertains to meaning within dreams is two fold. Firstly, that when the Pharaoh was being plagued by a dream, it was considered a top priority to have it interpreted. He implored every mystic he could towards that end. And though we may eschew this point as no more than a superstitious culture appealing to their superstitions, in the light of the second point, one must take pause. And the second point is the most obvious and important part of the tale — that Jacob's predictions came to pass.

So, if you're to take that account at face value, it would speak to the precedent being such that *before* Jacob ever correctly translated these men's dreams, others like him must have done the same. And to such a degree as to be considered not only the correct thing for the Pharaoh to seek, but so common that there were many people to choose from for the task.

It could be that in many of the cultures past, where these kinds of stories of predicting the future through dreams are found, that this practice happened much more often than was ever recorded for posterity.

Now, there arises another perplexing and disturbing paradox if you're to take for granted that some dreams can hold prophetic meaning. The idea that events can be known, or accurately predicted, before they happen brings into question every common preconception about *time* as a constant or even a universality. However this mind bending consideration may be less of an absurdity than most people think, as will be explored in the reality portion coming up.

Transdimensional Meaning

For the final consideration regarding meaning in dreams, we're going to take the focus in a meta direction when invoking the word 'meaning'. Instead of finding reason within the dreams themselves, what about the reason of dreaming at all?

We had asked the question earlier in this chapter 'why do we dream at all'? Perhaps that question is misguided in its enigmatic nature. Because, when considering the human body's need for sleep as a repair and mental decompression cycle, it *does* seem unnecessary. But weren't we proposing a dualistic view of the self? Could it be that the rationale for dreaming has far less (if anything) to do with the body side of our dual existence and more (if not entirely) to do with the consciousness side?

What we're proceeding to explore will widen the realms of possibility *far* beyond the boundaries of what can be scientifically reduced or rationally proven. Because, the areas I'm attempting to trespass into are held firmly behind the veil of sleep and the mysteries that abound behind it.

To set the stage once more before wandering into the abyss beyond what we can easily observe, I prefer to think about what we consider our universe to be as almost entirely (and perhaps necessarily) bound within the human spectrum of perception. And, as was explained early into this portion, that is likely a narrow band of the total reality happening around, through and within us at any given moment. It was proposed in chapter two that the consciousness portion of ourselves, that part that science has little to no answers or purpose for, could in fact be in large part exogenous to the physical side of our duality. Not so far removed as to not be constrained or affected by the physical, but distinct enough that it perhaps more natively resides (or originates from) some other part of our total reality that exists outside the biological spectrum of perception.

To call back to our analogy of the radio and the signal it receives, the signal is incredibly real. It is as real as the radio that receives and transmutes it into sound so that we can biologically interpret it through our ears. But we cannot see or even detect the signal without the radio acting as an intermediary translator of what is otherwise invisible and would remain completely unknown in its absence. I propose that so too does there exist some portion of reality (call it a plain or a dimension or a realm) that exists in synchronous or symbiotic relation to and within our perceivable reality.

In fact, I would further propose that there are many such intersecting unseen portions of reality that regularly intersect with what we experience as our human existence. In that light, perhaps what is happening at night during our nocturnal physical repair cycle, is a partial experience of those ethereal parts of reality that cannot be perceived in our waking state where the body rules our perception. It could be that in this state, the strange and seemingly unnecessary REM cycle where dreams occur, our consciousness that's typically held fast to our bodies loosens in some sense that allows for it to brush against parts of reality where signals exist, are born and perhaps even commune one to another.

In that sense, the dream state may perhaps be more aptly described as a dream dimension. Some part of reality that is as real and important to consciousness as the waking world is to our physical bodies. We posed the paradox earlier regarding the physical danger that REM presents to the body. How, during this portion of the sleep cycle, our bodies drift off the baseline of necessary internal heat and dysregulate to such a degree while in REM to oblige the counter balancing portion called NREM for the safety of the body. We asked how this could be beneficial to us as an organism considering evolution would demand the loss of such a detrimental state by dint of fitness selection over time. And as is witnessed in many other simpler animals, dreaming seems to exist there too.

Could it be that our consciousness, although entangled inextricably to our physical self, also requires a respite from the daily experience of our dualistic lives? That we psychically benefit to allow for the consciousness side of our selves to meander and stretch itself within the otherwise imperceivable dimensions that resonate more naturally against its core substance?

If this were the case (or something to this effect), dreams become a much wider and vibrant space for us to consider than just that of some nonsensical nightly psychological hallucination. It could be that an entire realm (as real as invisible signals through the air) exists in parallel and in subsistence with our physical spectrum of reality at all times, day and night. Though at night, we are able to interact with and within it by way of the piece of our being that may, in large part, be native to it's 'frequency' or 'substance'.

Many different religions (particularly the Eastern ones) speak in some way of such a parallel realm. In the Hermetic and Buddhist traditions, they label it the 'Astral realm' or 'Astral plane'. This is a portion of our total reality that is accessible through dreaming. But, also, through dedicated meditation. As such, entire practices have been laid out with the sole intention of purposely accessing the Astral realm. This is often referred to as Astral projection.

One popular Buddhist passage speaking to this kind of practice says the following:

> *"When their mind has become immersed in*
> *Samadhi like this, they wield the many kinds of*
> *psychic power; multiplying themselves and*
> *becoming one again; going unimpeded through*
> *a wall, a rampart, or a mountain as if through*
> *space, diving in and out of the earth as if it*
> *were water, walking on water as if it were*
> *earth, flying cross-legged through the sky like a*
> *bird, touching and stroking with the hand the*
> *sun and moon, so mighty and powerful,*
> *controlling the body as far as the Brahma*
> *realm."*

Drawing your mind back to the previous chapter, you'll notice (as I have in these studies) the stark similarities between the experience I had breaking out of my final sleep paralysis episode and my self 'leaving' my self. Floating effortlessly through the air simply guided by my intentions. I can't help but to make the connection and note the comparison between my experience and the practices that purposefully work to attain the same state.

In the sleep paralysis example I am in a state that completely precludes my ability to move my body. It's essentially a physiologically predetermined version of what monks spend hours working towards achieving. That is, a separation between mind and body while in a waking state. Through the determined efforts of meditation, practitioners learn to focus themselves solely on the consciousness side of their being, to the exclusion of their physical side. And, in their tradition, this effort can lead to the ability to functionally and intentionally move (or project) their consciousness (or Astral body) out of their physical selves to "[go] unimpeded through a wall, a rampart, or a mountain as if through space".

Much of the traditions, practices and religions that speak of these things consider it their highest goal to be able to 'ascend' or become 'enlightened' to the point of fully existing on a higher plane or realm of reality. Though this isn't meant as an argument for Buddhism or Hermeticism, through an exploration into them and other beliefs that look deeply within these topics, it becomes clear that there is and has been a universal human experience here that is broadly ignored or dismissed in modern Western orthodoxy.

Besides the very real possibility of finding the true purpose of dream ing, there may exist an entire facet of our reality that's otherwise being detrimentally ignored. A universe within a universe that coexists with what we recognize as our waking reality. And that opens its arms to us at the moments of our least attachment to the physical to welcome new and expansive realities available only within the ethereal.

Coming into our final chapter on consciousness, you will start to notice how this topic and that of the next portion —

reality — will both blend together and broaden out from many of the concepts and constructs that are shared by both.

9

BELIEF & DREAMS

"The future belongs to those who believe in the beauty of their dreams."

— ELEANOR ROOSEVELT

P erhaps the most commonly used form of the word *dream* refers not to the unconscious state we've covered so far, but to the yearning or longing for a future outcome.

This may, in comparison, seem like a more trite use of the word considering the expansive thoughtscape previously explored, but, as will become apparent in this final chapter on consciousness, there may be a power in this form of dreaming that doesn't get the respect it should. Particularly as we start to explore into the next portion's focus on reality.

———

You hear it as far back as your childhood: *"follow your dreams"*. It's a well worn phrase that likely loses its meaning as you grow up. Perhaps, in the process of maturing and finding your place in the world, you'll not only lose the meaning in this saying but a belief in it altogether.

There's something to the belief that you have the ability to set your own goals with the possibility of achieving them that is more than important, it may be a force unto itself. This force, or ability, or latitude through which we may access untapped potential has been a curiosity in many different arenas throughout time, culture and religion. And perhaps, as we delve into its citations and examples, you may find in them the requisite seed of belief necessary to open to you a new wondrous realm of possibility and potential.

Mind Over Matter

The idea of 'mind over matter' has been around for a long time. It has been explored through all sorts of religious practices and meditative endeavors, but typically, is counted as nonsensical in today's western society.

Stories of mothers lifting a vehicle off of their children who were pinned by it are commonplace folklore today but will just as quickly be dismissed by a critical mind as such. How would such an impossible feat of strength occur? Could the power of the mind legitimately overcome the laws that govern our physical reality?

We're going to explore into some of what we know and some of what we don't know around these sorts of assertations, starting with a physical anomaly you've probably heard of before — the placebo effect.

It may seem like a matter-of-fact thing to those who understand this effect, but as we start to unpack and explore some shocking case studies, the idea of mind over matter begins to become not only possible, but perhaps, powerful.

In Japan, researchers ran a study meant to qualify this effect in regards to a physiological reaction within its participants. They took 57 high school aged boys and blindfolded them. They then told the boys that there were two leaves being used in this study to test their effects on human skin. One was the leaf of a Lacquer tree, which they explained has a similar effect on human skin as a poison ivy leaf. The other was a leaf similar in size and shape but totally innocuous in comparison.

Once blindfolded, the researchers would go to each boy and perform the same test. They told them they were rubbing their right arm with the Lacquer leaf and the left arm with the innocuous leaf. Most of the boys' right arms broke out in a predicable rash, while nearly all of their left arms had no reaction.

You might wonder why *any* of the boys' left arms would have a reaction at all. Well, what was actually happening in the test was an important psychological trick. When they told the boys the leaf on their right arm was the Lacquer leaf, it was actually the innocuous one! And so they did with the left arm, telling them the leaf was innocuous while in fact rubbing it with the Lacquer leaf!

Living in a world of physical cause and effect, such an outcome seems startling and confusing. How could it be that simply by dint of suggestion, a predictable physiological reaction was reversed?

Another similar experiment was conducted on asthmatic patients. In that study researchers had every participant inhale a gaseous vapor they were told was an irritant that would flare up their asthma. Around half of the participants began to have breathing problems with some even progressing to full blown asthma attacks!

As it would turn out, the vapor was nothing more than an innocuous nebulized saltwater concoction that was not capable of bringing on such reactions. But, when they did, those who *had* such reactions were offered a medication to alleviate their symptoms, and all of them immediately recovered. Imagine their surprise when they found out that the medication was the exact same nebulized saltwater vapor!

In both cases, researchers were witness to another similar, but diametri cally opposed, effect to the placebo effect — the Nocebo effect. In the case of the placebo (meaning "I will please" in Latin), something that should have either a neutral or harmful effect has a beneficial one. While, with the nocebo effect (meaning "I will harm" in Latin), something that should have a neutral or positive effect has a detrimental one. All of which seems completely contingent upon the psychology or belief of the participant involved.

The placebo effect is so well accepted within the sciences that when running a placebo controlled test (where two identical pills or treatments are given to everyone in the study, but no one knows if they got the placebo or the pharmaceutical), it's imperative that neither side suspects what they received or else it may taint the outcomes, whether they guessed correctly or not.

There's also a well understood notion in sports psychology that the belief in an athlete's ability to perform, or conversely, the disbelief in the same tends to lead to outcomes that match. The inner thoughts they have, become in essence self fulfilling prophecies. But how much more compelling is it to find out that, beyond simply unlocking latent potential skills, the power of the mind can actually determine a physical condition despite the biology meant to restrain it to a contingent result? It's as if thought can, to some important degree, inform the very matter around and within us.

What other ways can a person use the power of their mind to affect their reality? Perhaps one of the most popular examples of this ability is a Dutch man by the name of Wim Hof, colloquially known as 'The Ice Man'.

Hof has made a name for himself in the practice of a specific breathing technique he's dubbed the "Wim Hof Method" that includes a significant degree of meditative qualities in its use. Hof even claims that his technique can reduce symptoms of diseases like rheumatoid arthritis, multiple sclerosis and Parkinson's. Beyond that, he has personally used the technique to set or break Guinness World Records in a number of categories as they pertain to the resistance of 'cold effects' on the body.

One such record was held for length of time spent swimming under ice, while another was held for length of prolonged full-body contact with ice. Remarkably, he even holds a record for running a half marathon (13 miles) barefoot, wearing only shorts, over ice and snow near Oulu, Finland. A feat that he completed in a time of 2 hours, 16 minutes, and 34 seconds!

Several scientific studies have been run on him to try and determine how it's possible to do these things that would kill other people if they attempted them. In 2014, a paper was published in PNAS (The Proceedings of the National

Academy of Sciences of the United States of America) titled "Voluntary Activation of The Sympathetic Nervous System and Attenuation of the Innate Immune Response In Humans". In this paper, the authors stated:

"In conclusion, we demonstrate that voluntary activation of the sympathetic nervous system results in epinephrine release and subsequent suppression of the innate immune response in humans in vivo. These results could have important implications for the treatment of conditions associated with excessive or persistent inflammation, such as autoimmune diseases."

Another study, in 2018, that was published in the journal NeuroImage, titled "Brain over body–A study on the willful regulation of autonomic function during cold exposure" came to the following conclusion:

"Our results provide compelling evidence for the primacy of the brain (CNS - Central Nervous System) rather than the body (peripheral mechanisms) in mediating the Iceman's responses to cold exposure."

In these and a number of other such studies into the man, whether or not the researchers came up with a physiological mechanism, they all seemed to nod to the fact that he has accessed the ability, through the power of will, to do something that should be impossible.

Mind Over Future

So far, we've discerned a surprising amount of control to which people have demonstrated in the use of their mind to counterintuitively affect their physiology. But what does this have to do with dreams in respect to the setting and achieving of one's aspirations? The former is going to lead towards the latter in, perhaps, an abnormal manner. A direction that may not seem obvious or possible, but for when its in respect to what is been noted so far with mind over matter, and also what we are soon to dive deeply into regarding reality itself.

One such facet of reality (that will come up in further chapters) is the immutable fact that our existence, as we perceive it in real time, functions only in the present. It seems derivative to say it, but our entire existence as we experience it is *only* really in the present moment.

The past is nothing more than our memories or records of the former present. Even if we watched video footage of our past, we would still only experience that recounting during the present, which itself would immediately thereafter become the past.

In what is a mirror image of that dynamic, the future is nothing more than our estimation, prediction, or aspiration of the present yet to be experienced. While the past can never be experienced again, so the future can never be experienced at all. Due to the linear arrow of time, everything is always (as far as we experience it) only an indefinite cascade of present moments.

Being that the majority of our reality is parsed through the aforementioned narrow sliver of human perception, this parsing is further narrowed (or at least skewed) by an erroneous holistic perception of time between an ever degrading past and an illusory (if not entirely fictitious) future.

It's been discovered already that our mind, by dint of conscious thought, can remarkably affect our biology. Far more so than many even realize it can. Being that those dreams we set for ourselves are by nature in the future, and that the future itself is an illusion of the mind, to what degree can our mind affect the future in regards to the dreams we have for it?

In one sense, it's a matter of fact that our present actions lead in summary to the outcomes they cause. But that's not exactly what I meant when I pose the previous question. There are going to be concepts and practices in the *reality* portion upcoming that will explore possibilities that suggest we may have a shockingly broader ability to not just predict, but *project* the future.

In a similar sense, like those hyper confident or hyper doubtful athletes tend to bring their perceived outcome to pass, belief seems to hold a variable power when applied liberally to a dream. And maybe, in the Sam Harris sense of a derivative universe subject only to an infinite summary of variables, belief simply leads one more reliably to those necessary variables to fulfill set dreams. But, perhaps, the total reality we exist in is stranger than we fully understand. And as we more widely consider possibilities relegated to the impossible, therein may lie a function of a paradigm left unrealized where dreams are as relevant as reality... and where reality itself is dependent upon *us*.

PORTION II: REALITY

"Ontology can be an ontology of difference... where what is there is not the same old things but a process of continual creation, an ontology that does not seek to reduce being to the knowable, but widens thought to palpate the unknowable."

— Gilles Deleuze, via Todd May

SECTION 1: HUMAN REALITY

10

PERSONAL REALITY

"The difference between fiction and reality? Fiction has to make sense."

— TOM CLANCY

F rom the moment of birth our reality is a mystery each person must solve. And the faster the better, because our ability to thrive within it is contingent upon an accurate assessment.

But as was proposed at the beginning of this book, the vast majority of that critical assessment is necessarily bound within the constrains of our major five human senses. These, themselves, must be discovered and mastered as they interact and react with the reality we continue to explore.

Upon achievement of this critical learning stage of early life there commonly proceeds a much longer stage (in many cases the remainder of one's life) where we more or less surf upon the previously acquired necessities for a human to thrive without any consideration of whether or not our total reality extends beyond it.

And why should such consideration matter to us? As a human, if you understand all of the relevant and actionable infrastructure necessary to get through each day, why would matters beyond that paradigm be of concern? In a general sense, they wouldn't. But, in a peculiar sense, they do.

There seems to exist in us not only the capacity, but the longing to further reach beyond what is the bare minimum that evolution would require us to grasp for the simple task of reproduction. This longing comes from a place that feels intrinsic if not native to something other than the reality we've learned or been taught to see us through a basic and prescribed human life cycle.

In the second portion of this book, we are going to reach deeply and broadly into many different (and sometimes frightful) possible versions of our total reality that will not only expand our place within it, but may even redefine or revoke the reality we've taught ourselves to live within up until this point.

It shouldn't need to be defined what we see the world as. Besides the differences within each of our individual experiences, most of a day in the life of any given human wouldn't fall (even in the most extreme cases) far beyond the boundaries of what we all perceive as possible or plausible.

But within, around, and between every normal day for us all there exists a remarkable and perplexing array of imperceivable facets of reality previously unknown to our former generations. As science and human ingenuity press on, fundamental aspects of the rudiments that make our existence possible are continually found. But even so, as these discoveries and concepts are continually aggregated into the whole of what we define our reality as, it seems we grow further from a holistic understanding the more we try to build one.

Simple actionable truths, like our inarguable relation to the material world, become disenfranchisingly opaque when further dissected. We think of ourselves, at any given moment, as a single unit or individual autonomous human. Broken down though, this simple, actionable, foundational truth becomes stranger than fiction.

Though we appear to have a unilateral command over our bodies, our bodies themselves are a mind-bendingly vast super-organism that consists of more than 31 trillion different cells! Each of which serves a particular purpose within the whole while simultaneously autonomously bound to its own internal superstructures of mechanisms and organelles.

If that's not enough, we as a human that consists of a galaxy of human cells within the confines of our individual bodies are in fact less human than we are non-human. Inside us all exists a symbiotic civilization of bacteria that, all told, outnumber our own human cells ten to one! Each of which are uniquely foreign in that they are not in any way human. It's no small thing to consider that a dys-regulation in that bacterial ecosystem will not only negatively affect our bodies, but can even affect our minds in the way of hormone imbalances that cause mood swings.

What's more, if you pull the scope in further upon the matter that our entire physical form consists of, what we find at the atomic level should disabuse anyone of the structure we've all presumed since childhood. That actionable and reliable conclusion that our physical structure is solid and broadly impermeable so that we won't fall through a chair when we sit down upon it. But upon a deeper observation of the nature of atoms, atoms themselves are less matter than they are void. That is to say, in between the neutrons, electrons and protons (as far as we can tell) there's nothing there. And *more* nothing than the mater that constitutes those fundamental forms! It's difficult to envision, but nothing means nothing. Not even air, being that air itself consists of atoms.

So, it wouldn't be incorrect to state that you are less you than you, *and* that the you you *are* is more void than not!

You can begin to understand what I meant earlier about a disenfranchising of the basic premises we've built our reliable paradigm of physical reality upon. But it gets much worse. The reality we know looks less and less like what we know the more we know about it.

For most people, the considerations already presented above are enough and as deep as they've been taught during their early educational stage of life. But there's a dimension below the atomic. And what we can relay back

from it thus far is counterintuitive to another level completely. Yet, so far as we can tell, it's the smallest reduction of our reality down to the most fundamental constituents that make up the substrate of physical existence — the quantum.

The very word "quantum" (pluralized "quanta") derives from the Latin root *quantus* which means "how much". If you want to quantify something, it requires a base unit to give an accurate answer. Therefore, the base unit cannot be divisible any further to allow for a quantitative response. When speaking to the quanta within physics, these are the very base a thing can be reduced down to. In the case of light, a photon is considered its quantum constituent. Within matter the quantum constituents are labeled as quarks, which appear as either an up-quark or a down-quark.

Besides the categorization and etymology, the study of the "quantum realm" and the utterly bizarre actions and effects within it have left those researching it more or less dumb-founded for the better part of the last 125 years. Leaving even Nobel laureate and notable theoretical quantum physicist Richard Feynman to famously say: "If you think you understand quantum mechanics, you don't understand quantum mechanics.".

Some of these enigmatic traits to quantum interaction go so far as to propose a level of contingency between whether or not we observe them. If you've heard the classic zen riddle "If a tree falls in the forest and no one is around to hear it, does it make a sound?", there exists a paradox in quantum mechanics that seems to mirror that observational query in a perplexing proposition called a *superposition*.

In quantum mechanics, a superposition refers to quanta that can either exist in one of two states, but seem to (as unbelievable as it may sound) exist in both states at the same time. More over, a quantum particle will appear in one of its two states *randomly* when an observer attempts to observe it! This paradox was famously analogized by renowned quantum physicist Erwin Schrödinger in the thought experiment called Schrödinger's cat.

In the Schrödinger's cat thought experiment you are told to picture a box. Within that box, you're told, is a cat. Presuming there's no sound or movement from the box, philosophically the cat inside can be equally considered both dead and alive. The only thing that will positively determine it to be one over the other will be the moment you can observe the cat.

This is a useful analogy when one tries to consider what seems to be an illogical quantum paradox. The hypothetical cat represents a superposition. And, although it (realistically) is only either fully dead or fully alive before you observe it, in the case of the quantum, it *really* is only by dint of observation that any quanta in question will be in one over the other possible state. What's more, that "selection" of state upon observation, appears to be fully random!

Schrödinger himself built a formula to present this absolutely counterintuitive portion of our reality mathematically called the Schrödinger equation. This is one of the foundational cornerstones that all theoretical physicists require to be able to work within quantum fields like particle physics or quantum computing.

So it's not off base to say that at the core of our observable universe, a rudimentary paradox exists whose solution is vitally contingent upon a third party observation of it.

In the light of this notion, found to be at the bedrock of man's accepted knowledge of the material, the lattice our daily human perception of the physical world is structured upon becomes obscure. How can it be that at the lowest reduction of matter, the attention of an entity — orders of magnitude above it in the physical — factors into the state of its existence? As if attention itself is a fundamental force we've not been solving for.

If that isn't unsettling enough of a consideration to accept, the further one explores into what other functions and para- doxes quantum theory suggests, the less one feels they understand what our total reality is at all! Especially as it's compared to the paradigm we all happily use to navigate the world in a day-to-day manner. It makes our 3D perception based mainly on the primary five human senses (while adequate for our purposes) appear ridiculously incomplete within the whole of reality.

One of those further functions of quantum mechanics is so strange in its application that Albert Einstein named it to reflect exactly that. He famously dubbed it "spooky action at a distance". This was the title given to

an observable and repeatable phenomenon that lead physi- cists to propose a mysterious mechanism they call quantum entanglement. In effect, spooky action can be observed when you affect a particle that's *entangled* with another. As you affect one, the other is effected. That wouldn't seem so spooky until you realized that this effect persists, it seems, regardless of how far apart you separate the entangled quanta. Experiments have been conducted that show this happening between two entangled particles that were across the world from one another!

So not only does the observation of the quantum affect its state, but entangled quanta will affect each other simultaneously regardless of distance. Upon that realization, the word spooky seems as apt as any. How it works, we don't know. But *that* it works should cause us to reconsider much of what we think the reality we're in is. It's akin to a re-writing of the rule book for a game you thought you knew how to play. Come to find, the rules were different the entire time. Even though, at the level of the game you were playing, you seemed to understand it.

Where quantum considerations attempt to *fully* disabuse us of our notion of reality is when it comes to something we reliably believe is more stable than even our practical understanding of matter — time itself.

In the latter paths of logic that quantum physicists find themselves walking down, something *so* illogical presents itself as if to force us to question everything we think is real. One of the most foundational and inescapable forces that all of the material world seems bound to is the linear arrow of time. Time moves in only one direction. Regardless of the fact that we only live in the present, the past is inaccessible to and unaffectable by us in any way. Or so all of human history and our personal experience would have us believe. But what if it turned out that not only can the past be affected by the present, but that it's contingent on it at a quantum level that runs diametrically opposed to what a linear arrow of time model would demand? Because this is exactly what is proposed to happen all the time with quantum interactions! Though this utterly mind boggling suggestion seems so far only to be relevant to the quantum realm, (that is to say, researchers debate whether or not quantum particles moving backwards in time realistically affect a change in

the past at the level of Newtonian physics, called *retro-causality*) it's broken open a previously impermeable absolute. The concept that time (at a variety of levels for a plethora of reasons) is fungible begins to turn inside out the entire construct we take for granted as our reality.

It's no wonder Feynman cautioned against presuming an understanding of the quantum. The base substrate of the physical universe seems to radically deny most of the knowledge we have been surfing upon to live our human lives on this earth.

Let's speak to time for a moment. We exist so utterly bound to it. In its uniformity and its inevitability. Try, for a moment, to consider what an existence unbound to time would look like. Honestly. Consider for a moment how that could be experienced. Even conceptually, the idea of existing without or unbound to time doesn't logically track for us as everything about what it is to be human is entirely contingent upon it. Not only in its inescapability, but its reliable consistency. A minute is exactly a minute. A second is always exactly a second. Or is it? Something happened in 2015 that confirmed a theory birthed one hundred years before it.

In 1915, Albert Einstein published his ground breaking theory of general relativity. Through this theoretical framework, much of what was previously accepted in the study of physics (namely Newtonian physics) was radically re-imagined. Among many facets of this new framework was the proposal of a fundamental connection between the concepts of space and time that Einstein simply called spacetime. This concept was proposed not only as a physical model but as its own dimension — the forth dimension. If the first three dimensions within space are length, height and depth, then the addition of a forth dimension — time — produces the theoretical manifold of spacetime.

This critical assertion proposed that as space is affected so too would an effect appear within time. But, in 1915, this was only theoretical. Everything seemed to track on paper, but how could it be proven or disproven to satisfy scientific rigor? It took until the 1960, but an experimental mechanism was constructed to try and detect this causal interaction between space and time. It's called the Laser Interferometer Gravitational-Wave Observatory (LIGO).

To understand how it works, first you must understand what they are trying to detect with it. Because, if Einstein's theory of spacetime is correct, a cosmic event massive enough to significantly bend space by way of extreme gravitation would also bend time in kind. Something like the collision of two black holes, being drawn together by their enormous gravitational pulls, upon the collision of their event horizons should produce a massive gravitational wave. This wave should carry on in all directions of space outwardly from the incident and affect time in one of two ways depending on what part of the wave hits the more placid spacetime it's traveling through. It should either compress space and time or stretch space and time. The LIGO observatories (one being built in Washington state and one in Louisiana) both test for either a stretch or a compression of space by firing lasers down two perpendicular kilometer long corridors in a way that would detect if the space along that track was ever slightly stretching or slightly compressing. What's more, both locations work in tandem so as to act as a redundancy were an event to occur. If a detection happened at one location and not the other, it would be considered a glitch or mistake. If a detection happened at both locations simultaneously but the values were different, it would be considered a coincidence. But if both locations simultaneously detected equivalent stretching or compressing of space, it would be considered a legitimate detection of a gravitational wave.

This brings us to September 14th, 2015. One hundred years after Einstein published his theory proposing the forth dimension of spacetime, a detection of a gravitational wave occurred. After all of the due diligence was satisfied at both stations, the announcement was made that the first ever gravitational wave was detected. The scientific world rejoiced as the theory of general relativity had its first major proof of concept in the physical world. But what's even more important is the fact that as space was witnessed contracting so too did time. Between 2015 and 2017, as all the gravitational waves from a proposed collision of black holes some 100 light-years away passed through our solar system, everyone on earth experienced time slightly faster.

Though the effects of that dilation were imperceivable, the precedent it proved was that time itself is malleable. What has always been considered

a constant was proven to be fungible. This consideration, now a proven scientific fact, brings into question the total malleability of time. And to come back to our original proposition about it, leaves open the possibility that it may not even be universal within our reality. For if there's a part of our reality where there is no space neither would there be time.

And though that's an obtuse thought that slaps any physical construct of the universe in the face, perhaps our perceivable reality is less *real* than we think, and upon further exploration, is more of an illusion than we know. More can be said and examples presented that further build the strange case for human reality, but suffice to say, as the lens is pulled in or out upon it; the more we discover the less we know.

In the next chapter we will move from physical reality to another disturbingly uncertain and utterly fungible pillar of our human perception of what's real — history.

11

HISTORICAL REALITY

"History is a combination of reality and lies. The reality of History becomes a lie.

The unreality of the fable becomes the truth."

— JEAN COCTEAU

M uch of what we learn about reality in this life is given to us freely. It doesn't require experience or exploration of our own, which is often a useful exchange for the sake of efficiency. Why learn everything through trial and error if the end result could be given to you by someone else who's already done the work?

Not only is this method of education efficient, but necessary if you hope to catch up to the societal expectations of a useful citizen. Though one of the intrinsic trade offs of having previously discovered knowledge given to you without your personal experience in the discovery process is a requisite amount of faith in its accuracy.

Among the most heavily saturated aspects of our reality, when it comes to the acceptance of unexperienced knowledge, is History. This is because we didn't experience all of it personally. Even if we wanted to, the best we have for learning about or from the past is entirely relegated to records and memory. Much of which are not of our own making.

It's because of this unavoidable fact that nearly every part of anyone's understanding of the past is thoroughly reliant upon faith. Many people don't even realize this fact, but all of us, most certainly, have an extremely distorted understanding of the past. And what's more, this distorted understanding greatly informs our perception of the reality we exist in.

By the end of this chapter you may have a wholly different opinion about history than you did before you began, and your entire view of reality in general may shift along with it.

What is history?

Most people learn about history through a culmination of exhaustive and explicit facts. These facts are passed down to them from experts like teachers, professors, and historians. Many of us take pride in our acquisition of entire volumes of historical quotes, tales, and texts to be recounted to others as intriguing facts about times long past.

But when you consider what any past event is (when transmitted forward for posterity), a shocking degree of presumption appears at every level.

At the level of those researchers whose job it is to discover the past, upon examination, their profession is more closely akin to the act of archaeology than it is a simple recitation of historic facts. Take any individual focus be it a time period, a culture, a civilization, or a specific individual; it goes without saying that historians can only uncover what they know through singular discoveries as they're discovered. However it is that the information about a time or people was able to be translated through time, that level of understanding is analogous to a paleontologist unearthing and piecing together disparate chunks of a fossil in the hopes of approximating a holistic picture of a time they never experienced.

As an analogy, long extinct life forms are a useful parallel. For example, there existed a long extinct species of shark called a Megalodon. This creature was considered to be an apex predator in the time it lived and is the largest shark species ever discovered to date. If you were to research what is known about the Megalodon, you'll come across entire studies and lengthy documentaries that explain their range, diet, life span, proclivities, temperaments, and even the reason for their eventual demise. By the end of this educational process you could walk away with a relatively robust understanding of an animal no human has ever seen before. You may even be considered an expert on it after a long enough, highly dedicated focus to the subject.

It may surprise you to find out though, that everything we "know" about the Megalodon has all been extrapolated and distilled from one single remnant of them: a tooth. Megalodon teeth are the only thing that remains of them at all. Nothing else. Every fact, tale, and conclusion is entirely drawn from that singular vector point.

You may ask, "Why's that an issue? There are highly proximate creatures today, like the great white shark, that have nearly identical teeth but for the size of them. What's the problem with an assumption based upon this extrapolation?". The problem is two fold, and I'll start with a specific example first.

In the 20th century, many of the ancestral predecessors to modern man were discovered and categorized into scientific fact. One of which, much like the Megalodon, came from the discovery of a single tooth that was recovered through barter in China at a remote confectionery. An entire recreation of this new subspecies of human — named *Hesperopithecus haroldcookii hominoidea,* or Nebraska Man — proceeded and was lauded by scientific journals for many years after the discovery. But five years after this remarkable discovery, the tooth that spawned it was re-examined and found to be, in fact, nothing but a pig's tooth.

Now you may (like many scientists since) look at this story as less of a problem and more of an example of good science self correcting over time. But the incorrectness of the story isn't the point. This brings me to the second part of that two fold problem examples like this and the Megalodon exemplify. Namely, that during the time between the discovery of this historical remnant and the realization of a critical error (in the case of Nebraska Man), human reality was built around a series of academic presumptions that everyone who learned of them simply absorbed as unquestionable fact.

This is the catch twenty-two that plagues all of history as a study and as an education. The entirety of what can be known comes down to a story you're being told to take as fact, whether the story is written by paleontologists about extinct animals, by archaeologists about extinct civilizations, or even by the records of those who actually lived through the events we study.

The latter consideration may seem a step too far. Direct, first hand accounts of an event (to a historian) are the gold standard of historical understanding. How could they too be a fabrication based on limited evidence? Well, if you consider that question for a moment, you may answer it for yourself.

If you were to categorize historical knowledge into two columns, one could be stories based upon evidence, and the other stories based upon stories. Because what more is the transmission of a remembered experience through writing than a story being told by the author? Without even presuming any incredulity upon the person writing, the best one can hope for from them is an opinion based upon a memory of their experience.

The opinion part of that transmission is inevitable, as a necessary filter between memory and the words chosen to relay it must be passed through. And that filter is fully dependent upon the writer's personality and proclivities at a conversational level. But, beyond that, the memories them-selves — *even* if the event they're writing about *just* happened — are so utterly flawed and tainted by our human medium of recollection as to limit our access to the total picture as it happened.

These days, in a court of law, eye witness testimony of an event is held in lower esteem than a video recording of the same event. The emotions, reasoning in the moment, and the degree of accuracy a virtual memory in our heads is colored by, can be so extreme as to paint an utterly inaccurate picture even from a first hand perspective of the event.

What's worse, people are incredibly prone to re-imagine an event after it's happened to try and reconcile the inaccura-cies their memories have of it. Creating a process of justifi-cation that can not only be wrong but even guided into a prescribed recollection by an outside force. Be it a person using leading questions in an interrogation or cultural pressures that guide a memory down an acceptable path, regardless of the reality of the actual event.

Again, I don't point these things out as an indictment upon any individual or even people in general, but they're meant to show how even the most reliable texts passed down through the ages must necessarily be riddled with incorrect information, regardless of how they found their way into the history books.

But it's by way of this realization, that a fundamental piece of our total human perception of reality is uncovered. And it's not about what information we're given, or even how it comes to us by. It's that all human transmission of understanding and knowledge is nothing more than an intricate construct of reality — that we each build based upon information we receive — and subsequently take on faith to be true.

At the level of individual perception of one's present reality — every single portion of the personal construct we've built ourselves through aggregation of inexperienced information is, realistically, an incomplete illusion meant to serve as the backdrop of the world around us. They are the stories that give comfort to an otherwise chaotic and confusing reality.

And there's nothing unnatural or unbecoming to believe the stories we're told, or even the stories we tell ourselves. In fact, when you really break it down, there's nothing *more* natural than story. Story is the only way humans communicate at all. Not only when it comes to communicating the past, or the present into the future, but every single part of how information is relayed between people is a form of story telling. Whether it is a historical story or an interpersonal story. Whether written or spoken. Even the words, letters, digits, sounds and symbols used to convey them — every part of that hierarchy of communication relies on a story that makes the information attempting to be transmitted make sense to another person.

In that sense, storytelling is biologically the only mode we have for attempting to relay our thoughts and intentions from one person to the next. But it's so important to recognize that that is what's happening in these processes. Because every single one of the prepackaged, fabricated and prescribed systems, worldviews, and lifestyles we are given to rely on in life are each curated to set particular parameters meant to lead you to a certain framework of belief to build your reality upon. And, we *must* build our reality upon *something*.

Life is a difficult and never ending discovery process of what we are, how we survive and efforts to improve our understanding of each. It's no wonder we all accept versions or portions of reality given to us by someone we trust based on faith.

When one strikes out to question or restructure parts of that framework, it becomes immediate evident that everything we've taken for granted was at several points the result of someone else doing the same thing. And though great wisdom can come from observation of other's explorations before us, wisdom itself requires a framework upon which to rest.

In consideration of everything above, though you require a historical framework to translate your reality through, no single historical under- standing or even belief system can possibly be considered as right. And certainly not to the exclusion of all others that (in their own application) serve as critical infrastructure for many people who use them to find their way through reality as they perceive it.

You may then ask the obvious and disturbing question: "To what degree can the reality we all live within be subjective to the individual?". As we move into the final chapter on human reality, we will dig into exactly that question. By the end of it, you may (as I have) stumble headlong into an idea that's as current as it is ancient — that reality, as we perceive it, may not exist at all.

COGNITIVE REALITY

"Reality is created by the mind. We can change our reality by changing our mind."

— PLATO

I n the previous chapter, we focused upon the issues and malleability of historical reality. The primary point revolving around a necessary amount of faith one needs to put into any information you pick up without your own personal experience in it. Near the end of this focus though, even the portion of your reality built through personal experience started to become hazy, as the mind itself is a highly efficient story fabrication

machine.

Now lets look specifically into that machine. Its method and its product. Because what we gain from its function is not only obviously critical for our survival but also critically imperfect by nature. Though, as we'll discover, perfection of its perception may not even be possible or necessary in the broad strokes. And for the amount of time and effort spent arguing over inherent, transcendental truths, we may simply be missing a major point to our perception of reality.

———

Inside the mind of every person exists a virtual reality. Its a construct of the layout and perimeters we believe the sandbox we exist in adheres to. That construct is built over time through the processes we've covered in the last two chapters. And as was made evident in them, those perimeters are anything but uniform. In fact, the virtual reality inside the minds of each individual person on earth is unique to a fascinating and important degree. Although we believe we're all living out a different vantage of the same paradigm, to a large degree, we aren't.

Nothing has made this more vividly clear in our present age than the advent and refining of social media platforms. The entire viability of their model relies upon a hyper-accurate assessment of each user's unique characteristics, proclivities, and a predictive level of likely actions for each that can be sold to companies for the purpose of high ROI (return on investment) advertisement. In the pursuit of this aim, extraordinary AIs have been built that utilize data aggregation algorithms whose purpose is to built a virtual "avatar" of each person based off of their social interactions on the platform. The avatars that are built in this manner can on average have *thousands* of unique attributes based upon your interactions. Think about how many unique, mental attributes you can name about yourself. If it's more than a dozen, that would be impressive. But (at the point of two thousand plus unique metrics about your behavior) the resolution these avatars have when put to work in a sales arena is staggering. And, more to the point, get *more* unique as more data points are added.

This is a useful proxy when considering how we, as humans, cognitively aggregate data we take in for the purpose of building an avatar of what the reality is that we live within. As the number of data points increases, so too does the resolution of the avatar of our reality. But just because the resolution increases, this doesn't mean that the accuracy of the resolution increases in kind. This can be a simple misunderstanding when considering these large scale cognitive processes. Because what's actually happening as more data is being inputted into systems, like a powerful AI or our own minds, isn't simply a cataloging of data. In fact, strong AIs are built upon the same model as the human brain called a neural net. This form of data storage builds data into the system while using it to build the system out at the same time. In this branching and exponential method, every new addition to the system breeds a myriad of branches that pertain to the data but also (and importantly) pertain to the interaction of the new branches with the existing branches that the previously accrued data produced.

This method of learning is much less like an ontological framework of categories and much more like a harmony between a virtual galaxy of nodes. One helpful analogy that scientist and researcher Brian Roemmele cited is that of a hologram. That if one were to consider the way a hologram is produced in space, that is more like how memories exist within the neural network of our minds. The way you turn singular points of light into a three dimensional hologram in space isn't simply by adding more and more singular points of light to the system. What creates a hologram are the intersections that each tiny beam of light make against and throughout the total system of light beams. As one beam intersects another at a certain point in space, their interaction creates a sort of pixel in the total picture the entire network is producing. So too does the lack of intersections add to the total picture in the way of negative space for the purpose of depth perspective.

In a similar sense, you can imagine our biological neural nets are receiving new points of light (data) and their blending of (or exponential interaction upon) the existing system of previous points of light not only more highly resolves our perception of reality, but can change the total picture as we see it. Moreover, the order in which information is added to the system will change the reality of the individual differently than someone else receiving the same information because of the way and extent to which each of our individual neural networks have been built up to the point of that new addition. Similarly, it's in this way (how each of our social media avatars are unique) that our individual internal virtual realities all inevitably differ one from the next. To what degree they differ is an interesting question, and would depend entirely upon the people you are comparing. But significantly enough to materially affect the reality around us in shocking ways.

One such example may sound like fiction until you realize how real it is. Certain researchers and historians believe that the color blue didn't exist in the ancient world. Not that the color itself didn't exist but that human perception of it didn't exist, which (insofar as civilization is concerned), materially affected the reality of all our ancient forebearers.

This realization began with a scholar in 1858 by the name of William Gladstone who noticed, while studying ancient Greek texts, that there was no reference to the color blue. In Homer's *The Odyssey*, he described the color of the ocean as a "wine-dark sea". As Gladstone looked further into Homer's works, he noted all sorts of peculiarities around colors. The color of sheep and armor was defined as violet, while honey was cited as green.

And it would be strange enough if it were just one writer from just one era, but this pattern was expanded upon later by a philologist named Lazarus Geiger who noticed this across all cultures! From Icelandic sagas to the Quran, ancient Chinese tales to original Hebrew versions of the Torah — none of them had any description for the color blue. Even in the Vedic texts, that are replete with hymns speaking to the majesty of the sky, never once was the color blue mentioned. What's more (and importantly), none of their languages even have a word for it! Many of the descriptions found noted either the colors of the sunset in reds and yellows, or they would speak of the daytime skies as a gray or white.

Upon these realizations, Geiger began to catalog when it was in each civilization that a color started to be documented. In that effort, he discovered a pattern when the further you went back in a language, they would mention black and white, then red, and sometimes yellow. Greens would come later and blue was one of the last to appear if it ever appeared at all. In fact, the only ancient civilization that had a word for the color blue were the Egyptians. Who also happened to be one of the first civilizations that had a way of making blue dye for their clothes and paints.

Curiously, a researcher named Jules Davidoff recently went to the African country of Nambia in search of a particular tribe that still doesn't have a word for the color blue. Taking many of the members of this tribe and showing them a picture that had twelve colored squares in a circle, he told them that one of the squares was blue and the rest were green. Not one of them could perceive the blue square immediately and often not at all. For those who did pick it out, it was a strained effort and sometimes came after a couple incorrect guesses. I've seen this exact image, and the blue is vividly different than all the other green squares. It's not slight in any way, and anyone I know (even children) would pick it out ten out of ten times. Now, what's even more interesting in this case, is that this particular tribe happens to have many more words for colors of green than most other languages do. They replayed the experiment with another set of colored squares in a circle. This time they were all green, but one of the squares was a slightly different green and was in a different position than the blue square from before. In this case, every single tribe member immediately picked out the different green square as if it were the blue square from before that we could so clearly see. I also saw this exact image, and I chose wrong.

It's unbelievable to consider, but the very existence of entire colors (that should be universally visible to everyone by dint of the same biological hardware being used) may simply not exist in some people's cognitive perception of reality. In chapter two we talked about different animals being able to see colors we can't, but that ability was tied to biological differences. In this case our eyes are all human eyes. What differs is simply the knowledge of the concept of a color.

A fascinating suggestion arises out of this example. In the tradition of the stoic philosophers, ontological frameworks are built through consideration of the world around the observer. It is considered an effort in discovering a priori intrinsic truths that exist within our reality. In the twentieth century, a philosopher by the name of Gilles Deleuze proposed an entirely different model of philosophy. Whereas Plato or Aristotle may have considered it their goal to uncover transcendental truths that already existed in the universe, Deleuze considered truth (and any ontological frameworks built to support them) an act of creation not discovery.

Deleuze took many different counter culture views of reality. But the concept of creation in regards to the very truths of reality feels more like the malleability of a dream than that of the physical world. Though, given the fact that we just covered how the presence or absence of a word can fully determine whether or not someone can "see" a color, the Deleuzian suggestion begins to hold weight. For if a world view could exist without the color blue (that is only made visible by a predetermined neural lattice to support it), what does that mean about any truths we've accepted that are also contingent upon preemptive frameworks? And this, I believe, is what Deleuze meant by a creation rather than a discovery.

Now, you may ask, to what degree can our perceptions — these person- alized virtual realities we cast onto the physical reality — really affect the physical? And there's a real conversation there that would necessitate a case- by-case examination. Whether it's the ability to see a color, or our biological ability to force an unnatural change within our bodies via the placebo effect; how much of the world we live in, that we believe to be objectively true, is in fact subjective?

Deleuze brought forth another example of something we consider a universal constant that will call back to our previous exploration into human reality — that of time. We've covered the fact that our perception of time is only a phenomenon of the present. The past was shown to be largely a montage of highly subjective memories and viewpoints, whereas the future is forever intangible, existing in our mind, beyond physical grasp. But Deleuze questioned the present itself, the only reality we truly live in. He asked, when is the present that we live in? Is it this second? Is it half a second? Smaller? The question points out a paradox within our perception of the very present moment we exist. Because we can infinitely divide a moment in time, there actually *is* no moment to speak of. Instead of thinking of the present as a moment or unit of time, Deleuze proposed instead of thinking of the present in a way that's spatially tied to our physical reality. He suggested that the present we exist in is the exact intersection where the past and future meet. As if the epicenter of a black hole where we and our perception of temporal reality are locked, time itself (and our relativity to it) may not even be what we think of it as.

But surely, even though our temporal and spatial perceptions of reality may be skewed, inaccurate, and individualized, there *must* still exist a literal reality that remains unaffected by our perceptions of it. An objective substrate that, however misunderstood, exists in a universal and factual sense around us. A rock is experienced as a rock no matter whose hand you place it in. Its effects on its surroundings are predictable, testable and well understood regardless of whose perception of it may argue the fact. Our perceptions, be they physical, historical, or cognitive, are separate from its reality… Aren't they?

In the next few chapters the substrate of reality will not only come into question but the entirety of the system it's in. Because, there's another level of reality beyond our perception within it that (in a broad, meta sense) invalidates everything we think our existence even is. And it's at this level where the roots of all the great theologies, philosophies, and even sciences begin.

SECTION 2: SIMULATION THEORY

13

THE UNIVERSAL SIMULATION

"Life is not a problem to be solved, but a reality to be experienced."

— SØREN KIERKAGAARD

Of the different levels one can consider when observing and pondering our reality (like the material, the historical and the cognitive that we've already explored), one layer subsumes them

all. It's a meta level of existence that brings into question the entirety of reality as we know it.

Many different people, cultures, and beliefs have questioned this level of reality. Whether or not and to what degree the realm we exist in is real at all. In these modern scientific days, this area of consideration is relegated to a specific, colloquial term — Simulation Theory. Although the word "theory" is certainly misused in this context, there exists a surprisingly varied and robust field of thought in the philosophical, scientific, and theological spaces regarding a number of simulation constructs. Though few of them can be reconciled against each other, and none of them can be proven or disproven by nature, there is a throughline they all point to; that we deeply misunderstand what existence even is. And that the system we're in is not at *all* what it seems to be from within it.

In 1999, I was a high school kid living in British Columbia, Canada. Upon returning from a weekend camp in the spring of that year, a friend of mine told me about a film that had just come out in theaters. He seemed very excited to see it so I went with him, completely oblivious to what I was going to see. By the time I walked out of the theater that night my head was spinning. Not only had I *never* seen anything like it in the way of cinematography, but the greater concepts of the film left a lasting impression on me, and many others, when it comes to the idea of a systemic simulation of reality.

The movie was the Wachowski brothers magnum opus: *The Matrix*.

This film has so ensnared the individual psyches and collective zeitgeist of society ever since that people understand and reference *The Matrix* by name both in casual conversation and in clinical theses regarding simulation hypotheses. If ever the topic of a totalizing simulation was faux pas or ill-considered in popular culture before it, since then not only is the subject open for discussion, but entire careers have been built upon its possibility.

Perhaps the thinker who has spent the most time and effort to build out this space within the sciences is Oxford fellow and Swedish philosopher & mathematician Niklas Boström. When people use the term "Simulation Theory", they are referencing the work Boström has done on what he has coined the "Simulation Hypothesis".

Simulation Hypothesis

The core premise of this hypothesis centers around the idea of an ever nearing technological crossing of the Rubicon.

As technology continues to improve in the areas of hyper real visuals and experiences there is a hypothetical point where reality begins to blur between what is and isn't real. This inflection point is deemed the "uncanny valley".

With immersive video games and interactive online universes becoming more and more believable, vivid, and indistinguishable from reality, Boström states that at the very moment (called the simulation point) humanity can create a total and consuming universal simulation (like *The Matrix*), it becomes statistically likely that we ourselves are also within one.

Take a moment to consider what he means by that because the implications run deep. If humanity technologically evolves to a point where we can build an indistinguishably real yet fully simulated universe, then not only does it become possible that we're also within one, the chances that we are the first (or ancestor) civilization, is mathematically less likely than if we're not.

Many complex and enigmatic contingencies arise when you think of the implications that come with this paradigm. Firstly, not only would an indefinite series of simulations have to be proposed but they would theoretically each be a derivative and functionally parasitic part of the higher order simulation before it. Because, if we build a universal and self sustaining simulation within our reality, it relies on our reality to exist. Even if internally, it's unaware of our existence. And in the computational aspect of such a simulation there would necessarily be a minimum baseline of energy and informational power required from the parent reality to sustain the lower level reality it has built. This leads to the second limiting contingency to such a model, one that

Boström calls the computational "tower". Wherever the root ancestor reality lies, every single reality that gets produced after it (as you move proverbially up a tower that's building the next layer on top of itself) will be "smaller" or limited in comparison to the total reality that produced it. Beyond that, as each proceeding reality is simulated within the next, the requisite energy input into each system compounds backwards through the tower to the base reality. That exponentiality builds a total possible ceiling to the height of any computational tower.

Outside of the details and mathematical functionality (of which Boström has gone very deep into) other more philosophical questions appear as you consider the possible scenarios intrinsic to this hypothesis. For instance in the case of *The Matrix*, there was one base reality — wherein humanity had been conquered by machines they'd built — where the minds of all humans in the matrix were being ported in via hard wire connection to the brain. Two immediate questions arise if this were the model of the base reality in a computational simulation tower. Firstly, if we are not (as would be statistically the case) the base reality then would who we are be linked to a physical body that is actual and not simulated? Certain paradoxes present themselves if that's the case. Such as children being born into this level of reality. In 2021, there were statistically 4.3 children being born every second of the day. Either the rise and fall of total human numbers with every death and birth must perfectly match the parent reality (considering we are an avatar of a physical being in the base reality), or there are people in our level of reality being born that are strictly internal and not related to any physical being in our parent reality. That brings up the second of the two immediate questions in the matrix model of a simulation. If the computational tower analogy were to proceed from a base physical reality to a first level simulated reality, then the very next simulation within that tower (the one that would be built within the "Matrix" version of reality) would either be entirely populated by fully simulated people who have no direct connection to base reality, or they would become a second fractal projection of the base beings now two times removed. The first consideration brings an entire panacea of new predicaments regarding the first nine chapters on consciousness. While the second presents an eerie echo or redundant facsimile paradox that lead to a similar issue of consciousness where the ethics of every proceeding layer of reality lend to murkier and murkier conclusions.

Of course, it's most comforting to presume that we would be the base reality and that our trek towards the first totally simulated reality would indeed be a new precedent set. And although (in Boström's hypothesis) it's unlikely to say the least, let's take it for granted for a moment that we are. What is it that would necessitate that we even *do* build such a simulation? Or furthermore, that within that simulation they *too* would end up building their own? One of the ideas around this will preview some of the concepts that will later come up in the *purpose* portion of this book. It has to do with the odd community dynamics of humans as a species. Someone who's spoken often about this particular peculiarity is famed comedian turned podcast king Joe Rogan. He refers to this idea as the technological caterpillar.

Rogan contends that, at a large scale community level, human beings have an intrinsic and insatiable desire to innovate. And one innovation is never enough it only necessitates the next. In this fashion, humanity seems hapless in its communal efforts towards what seems to be the creation of a virtual successor. As computers are built that then build upon themselves (both internally and externally), it's an inevitable path towards a super- intelligence that utterly eclipses and likely succeeds us as the apex entities on earth. Thus, we as humans are merely the technological caterpillars building their proverbial silicon cocoon from which will emerge the next metamorphosis beyond humanity. If this intrinsic urge exists or existed in the base level reality, it would almost certainly lead towards the creation of an indistinguishable simulation of reality. And what's more, Boström would add the insight that at any point along the tower of simulations, this trek towards insatiable technological improvement could produce AIs that carry on the process regardless of any base level entity guiding or actuating it to. That is to say, anywhere along the way, every part of every hypothetical simulation may be simulations simulating simulations all the way down. Besides the base level humans (if in fact that's what they would be), physical beings like we consider ourselves may not be necessary to the building of a computational simulation tower beyond the first iteration. Realistically, with a strong enough AI, this may already be happening within present day AI constructs, to some degree, and we may not even know it.

So far, we've mainly been explaining Matrix style scenarios and Boströmian simulation towers. All of which speak to the theoretical *how* of a computational simulation. But what about the reality we exist in right now would lead one to suggest this as a synthetic reality opposed to a base level one? Well there are a variety of peculiarities that exist in our universe that (at the very least) should give one pause when observing them. As with any such observations rationality can dismiss them all in any number of ways. Though, in the same way the dream world can be justified away as nothing but nonsense, be wary not to over-rationalize away what could be clues into the greater secrets of existence.

Fractals

One of the standards of our material universe seems to be a rooting in practical and predictable patterns. In fact, humans as a rule tend to be pattern seeking by nature. But it's within nature that an intriguing set of patterns emerges once explored deeply enough. If one were to make the case for a simulated reality, finding logic within it would be a necessary expectation. But more so than the physical laws that seem to govern our reality, as with all coding and computer theory, patterns would be a constant and inevitable feature.

If you were to set out in the hopes of proving a simulated reality while *within* said realty, along the way you would certainly discover patterns that pertain to the logic of the system you're in.

In the 1980s, a Polish-born French American Mathematician named Benoit Mandelbrot was working for IBM. Mandelbrot found a personal interest in a certain set of enigmatic mathematical discoveries ranging from the early 1900s to his time. Each of these discoveries had something to do with an odd application of infinite paradigms discovered in nature and geometry. One such example was Swedish mathematician Helge von Koch's paradoxical triangle. He had discovered that one could add a symmetrical apex in the middle of each side of a triangle and theoretically repeat that pattern into infinity. The paradox of that thesis was that although the radius around such a geometrical shape never expanded (making it finite in size), the perimeter of infinitely added apexes never ended (making its perimeter infinite). This and other such geometric truths, such as the fact that a single line segment can be infinitely divided (remember the same contention that Deleuze had regarding time in the present), were deemed in mathematics as "monsters". Being that Mandelbrot was working at IBM he found himself with access to powerful (by 1980s standards) computers that he could use to crunch these "monster" equations. In so doing, he not only refined the equations into a set that defined them and their geometric standards (called the Mandelbrot set), but he redubbed these occurrences as "fractals".

In the Mandelbrotian sense, a fractal is something that no matter how far you zoom in on it or divide it into portions, it will continue to present with the same shape or pattern. This feature is found all over nature, particularly in branching patterns. Things like: river systems, lightning, trees, broccoli, walnuts, human brains and even the neural net found within them. In the colloquial sense, the term fractal can be invoked when viewing interconnected systems that house startling similarities as you move the lens from the macro to the micro regardless of scale.

And this particular pattern set isn't the only one like it that both appears and repeats throughout the universe. Going all the way back to the ancient Greeks, mathematicians like Aristotle and Pythagoras noted a divisional pattern both appearing mathematically and in nature they coined the divine ratio. Also known as the golden ratio or the golden mean, this ratio, when denoted as an irrational number, is called cj (pronounced "phi"). Phi, like pi, equals an endless number that never repeats, usually abbreviated to 1.618. The first historical reference to this concept dates back over 2300 years to Euclid (father of Euclidian geometry) in his book *Elements*. Versions of this ratio can be found throughout all sorts of ancient Roman, Mayan and Egyptian architecture, renaissance paintings, and most fascinating of all — nature. Structures like pine cones, nautilus shells, human finger prints and even cosmic nebulas and galaxies seem to mirror (although not mathematically exact) similar formations. From an artistic standpoint, many schools of thought consider it to be central in what the human eye deems as beautiful. Giving it another name, the divine proportion. Famous brand logos (like Apple's for example) are said to use the golden ratio in an effort to make them pleasing to the eye. On the practical side of applications this ratio has been utilized to effect in the modern fields of high energy physics, quantum mechanics and cryptography.

Another famous and similar set is directly related to the golden ratio, as solving for it retroactively will equate to phi — the Fibonacci sequence. This is another simple yet fascinating number set that continues on for eternity, while the truth of it is evident and binding at all levels. Examples of this sequence can be found in horticulture through a variety of plant structure including how a tree trunk branches out, the leaves of some plants and the pedals of some flowers. In the colloquial sense of the word, these structures ring of a fractal essence. Humans have found use for its structure in engineering too. Everything from computer data structures, sorting algorithms, to architecture and audio compression software.

Now the simple fact that these logical patterns are evident throughout the universe doesn't necessitate a simulation, per say. Some may make the argument that based upon the foundational principles that keep the universe in order (things like Einstein's cosmological constant or other intrinsic properties like strong nuclear force), one should expect to find logic within such a system. Simply patterns that form based upon the constraints of the system's parameters. What I am proposing is that, in a systemic sense, you would also expect to see such logical structures, patterns, and constants in any sort of simulating engine or coding infrastructure. And although vital logic and intricate parameters aren't exclusive to computing, this could be a logical fallacy on our part if we are actually in a simulation. Put another way, if one were to negate the similarities of our own computing infrastructures in comparison to the physical universe because said universe will inevitably have constants and patterns rooted in its physics; that negation appears as ignorance if in fact we are stating that *while* within a simulation. It's a perspective issue that stems from an assumption that we're *not* in a simulation. This is where justifications can overrule any suggestions of a simulated reality because they start from an *a priori* view that our reality is *not* simulated.

Keep the concept of fractality in mind as we continue throughout this book. It's something that seems (if not mathematically) colloquially ever present. As the lens of view is pulled deeply in or broadly out, it's truly shocking how much similarity exists at all levels.

While fractals may play a part in the logic or patterns of the system we're in, what about the illogical instances? There are a couple specific examples in the next chapter of very odd but seemingly universal hiccups or glitches in our reality that will again cause one to consider the reality of our reality by the end.

14

MANY WORLDS AND THE MANDELA EFFECT

"I regard the [many worlds Interpretation] as self evidently correct."

— STEPHEN HAWKING

I f the proposal of a simulated universe wasn't enough, as we follow the white rabbit down its hole on different versions of simulation hypothesis, things only grow bigger and wider in all directions.

There is a very active and cutting edge area of intrigue in quantum physics that leads to not only the possibility of a simulated universe but of a higher order simulated *multiverse*! And as with the previous chapters, once the ideas are laid out, there are certain peculiarities we all experience in life that make even more sense within this framework than they did without.

In chapter ten we introduced the basics of the quantum realm. Things that, upon inspection, appear absolutely counter-intuitive to the level of reality we exist at. Properties of quanta that affect their state, definition, location, and even direction in time can both exist simultaneously as well as be affected externally by nothing more than our observation of them. Many famous and talented physicists and mathematicians have spent the better part of the last century trying to understand and reconcile these utterly bizarre properties against our recognizable universe. In their frustrated efforts, a number of them have erected what some call the "first wall" between these levels of existence. That is to say, for lack of a reconciliation between human level and quantum level physics, they consider the two (although codependent) separate in the laws that govern each. Because of how many ways quantum mechanics seem to run against Newtonian and even Einsteinian physics, this first wall is a proposed distinction between the two levels wherein the physics of each don't follow from one to the other.

Although this is not a universally held belief. Other physicists like John Wheeler, believe that there is a union between the two in a number of fascinating ways. The very quest for such a unifying theory has been a goal of all theoretical physicists since Einstein's theories of relativity and special relativity were accepted. Einstein himself was trying, unsuccessfully, to rectify what seemed like a list of impossible paradoxes between these two levels of physics for the remainder of his life. Along this quest, Wheeler proposed a theory that (although it didn't unify the levels entirely) tore down the first wall between the quantum and base realities.

It all came back to a reimagining of what may be happening at the moment that quanta in a superposition "choose" a state to be in. As a reminder, quanta (take, for example, a single photon of light) can exist in a superposition between two definite states (like differing waveforms) that isn't just neither state, but literally both states at the same time. And like Schrödinger's cat, only defines itself as one or the other upon our observation of it. Perhaps one of the most baffling additions to this field from Wheeler was a proposed experiment to prove not only that the observation is what randomly defines what state a quanta will take, but that the observation isn't even bound by time!

In a now famously proposed experiment, it was discovered that an observer of an unobserved photon of light while in a superposition, could make an observation of it in the present that would affect it into a defined state in the *past*! This experiment, called the delayed choice experiment, used the light from a distant quasar as it passed a black hole to prove its hypothesis. Essentially, the light would act differently as it passed the black hole were it in superposition or in one of two defined right or left spinning waveforms. The only way it would choose a singular state over a superposition was if it were observed. The most interesting part of this experiment though, is that observations *that* deeply out into space (in the case of quasars, hundreds of millions of lightyears away) is literally watching the past. Any actions we see from earth have already happened approximately as many years ago as the distance they are away in lightyears. So everything we see has already happened eons ago. Using the quasar and black hole as a long distance version of the delayed choice experiment, researchers confirmed that upon them observing light that already passed by a black hole millions of years ago, it presented in a defined state! This proved that quantum observation can travel backwards in time.

This seems utterly inconceivable to anyone (like most of us) who holds a linear view of time as an incontrovertible constant. Einstein proposed that time could be slowed (or dilated) as one traveled closer to the speed of light, but the idea that random chance in the present could affect quantum action in the past was something else entirely. Because if we in the present can affect the past, then it goes to follow that those in the future can affect the present.

And before you go spinning off into thoughts of time travel just yet, there's that pesky first wall that states even though all this spooky stuff can happen at the quantum level, it doesn't follow into the level of physics that we reside in. Or... does it?

As more of the strange effects and properties of the quantum were being proposed and subsequently proven, hypotheses attempting to reconcile it with our level of physics were beginning to be written. This is where we begin into what many people may have heard of through various science fiction stories. Whether by the name of infinite worlds, parallel universes, or the more academically accepted Many Worlds Interpretation (MWI). And again, it all comes back to quantum duality in superpositions.

If you consider quanta in superposition (instead of holding two states at once) being a multiple choice question in a choose-your-own-adventure book, physicist and student of John Wheeler, Hugh Everett III proposed that instead of them choosing one state or the other upon observation that *both* states are set — but in different, branching *parallel* iterations of the universe. That may be hard to picture, but if you were to think of our reality as a branching fractal of time-lines (instead of as one constant system), this is what is proposed to be happening at each point that a quantum superposition chooses its state upon observation. This idea has been played with in pop culture in the Marvel universe between films like *Avengers: Endgame* and *Loki* television series. The major difference in comparison is, with the cinematic interpretations timelines fracture due to important events or choices of an individual, whereas in the quantum multiverse hypothesis, every single time a quantum state is determined, the determinacy that we see is only the state it chose in our timeline. The state it seemingly avoided was actually chosen in what then becomes a parallel timeline. Everett coined this action quantum decoherence, which would be the diametric opposite of a quantum superposition.

Godfathers of modern physics, like Albert Einstein and Niels Bohr, balked at the notion that the entire universe was essentially being cloned every time any quanta decohered. They simply wouldn't accept the absurdity of it (preferring the traditional Copenhagen interpretation) though admitted that the formulas Everett proposed in his thesis seemed to work. Due to the skepticism it received (and out of respect for the monolithic characters of Einstein and Bohr) Everett would tone down the wording of his doctoral thesis not to sound as though this was what he was suggesting.

Sixteen years later, in 1973, Everett's work would be picked up and championed by the next generation of upcoming physicists, namely, one Bryce DeWitt. Not only would DeWitt bring prominence to the thesis once more, he published it in a book titled "The Many Worlds Interpretation of Quantum Mechanics". Thus coining the phrase that is, now-a-days, simply abbreviated as MWI.

Today many physicists accept and work within the MWI framework. Even famed theoretical physicist Stephen Hawking said of it, "I regard the [many worlds Interpretation] as self evidently correct.". But how does this tie into a simulation hypothesis? In the book "The Simulated Multiverse" author, Stanford graduate and MIT Professor Rizwan Virk (who came from the video game and computer coding world) has an interesting suggestion about that. Cloning an entire physical universe, as we perceive ours to be, umpteen times every nanosecond throughout the universe with every quantum decoherence does seem absurd. Unless the universes being cloned were simply in an informational state that was a function of the total simulation we exist in. He cites Wheeler who himself stated that at the root of it all, everything is information. Virk proposes that the panacea of simulated realities these events spin off could be a computational function of a sort of "what-if" aspect of a massive AI structure. Something like an "a/b" test after every decoherence instance to either run or save a parallel doppelgänger universe. Towards what end is a fascinating question, but before we go there, the important part to note is the logic in such a proposal. As far as computation and information theory goes, it tracks as plausible.

One of the suggestions Virk lays out about the "towards what end" question I found quite interesting to imagine. The idea of a *prime universe* in which we exist, where the *what-if* test universes serve as ever present counter factual possibilities to be run so as to determine which of the binary options from each decoherence instance proves most beneficial to whatever prime directives were built into the master simulation as parameters by its architects. In theory, once the a/b test has been run, and the more appropriate universe decided upon, the favorable universe is the version that becomes our prime universe, whereas the less favorable one could either be stored as data or discarded altogether. And although such a computational task far exceeds our current technological limits, the logical process of it tracks quite nicely. One of the questions you may ask upon consideration of this proposal is "would these tests be run and completed so fast as for us not to notice in real time?". This question will actually serve well as both a segue into the next topics of this chapter as well as a foreshadowing of another possible answer to it in the next.

Déjà vu and the Mandela Effect

It's an odd sensation. When, in the moment, you feel like you've already experienced what's happening right now. Sometimes it's a phrase or the entire scene around you. Everyone's experienced that feeling we call déjà vu. Déjà vu seems to strike randomly and its unpredictability is an aspect of what makes it a difficult thing to test. Many different physiological and psychological explanations have been forwarded, although they're admittedly unconfirmed so far. Examples of physiological proposals are that perhaps there is a misfiring between the long-term and short-term memory in the brain and what you're experiencing feels like a long-term recollection when in fact it's never happened before. Another explanation some researchers forward is an unusual delay between the information being stored in memory and the relaying of the sensory organs tracking them. Though this is a difficult argument to make since any visual memory stored would *have* to be seen before it could be stored. It wouldn't make sense the other way around even if there was an uncommon delay from the eyes to the brain. Some of the psychological explanations tabled state that perhaps there is a latent dream that resembles the current situation. The experience of the situation sparks a vague recollection that trying to remember a dream elicits. Some psychiatrists suggest that it could be the results of a minor psychosis as déjà vu has a higher frequency in those with schizophrenia, anxiety and temporal lobe epilepsy.

The fact that so many different specialists present so many possible suggestions points to the degree of uncertainty that science has in this phenomenon on the whole. Though there are a few pharmaceuticals that can make them more common, they simply cannot be reliably studied. But beyond the difficulty inherent in their research, science will be the first to admit that they simply will not permit any non-physiological answer to it. And therein may lie the fallacy that could prevent our understanding of it.

To hearken back to The Matrix we touched on in chapter 13, there was a scene where the protagonist, Neo, saw a black cat walk by a doorway twice in short order. He coyly mumbled "Huh... déjà vu.". The entire team of heroes around him (who all understand the Matrix and its functions) froze. Trinity, the lead heroine, asks Neo what he saw. He told her about the cat that walked by and then another just like it. "Just like it, or the same cat?", she asked. At that point the team begins to scramble towards their objective as Trinity explains to a confused Neo that "Déjà vu usually happens when there's a glitch in the Matrix. It means they've changed something.". And sure enough, the system had been adjusted, while they were inside a building, to brick off all of the exists and windows, trapping them in it.

This scene speaks to the possibility within a simulated multiverse that Virk (through the efforts of Everett and DeWitt) suggests could be the result of what is a reconciling or "rendering" (perhaps even re-rendering) of the prime universe by way of an a/b conclusion being detected by someone in real time. Think of it like a save-state in a video game. If time is a consideration of the simulated multiverse, perhaps the blazing speed of the rendering to reconcile one of two quantum universal outcomes wasn't quite fast enough for someone to detect or remember the prime universe before it was reconciled into the other binary option. Or if time is *not* a consideration (which we'll dive more deeply into in the next chapter) and the system needn't be reconciling parallel universes at speed (more like a traditional video game safe-state), then déjà vu could be a re-loading of the universe back in time if there needed to be an adjustment at a certain point to prevent (or produce) a certain desirable outcome regarding the system's objectives or parameters.

This type of thesis is a much harder sell in typical academic conversations around something like déjà vu. But, that need not matter if, in fact, it turns out to be the case. And what's more, another very odd phenomenon fits this framework. One that, although some relegate it to conspiracy, has fascinated and perplexed many whom it's affected. Beginning with the researcher who first noticed it, Fiona Broome.

Broome herself says that she has a vivid and undeniable recollection of South African anti-Apartheid movement leader Nelson Mandela having died in prison in the 1980s. Memories that include seeing it in the news and watching the enormous funeral event televised thereafter. As it turns out, Mandela didn't die in prison, nor even in the 1980s. He would go on to live and become the president of South Africa from 1994-99, dying years later in 2013. After this personal revelation, Broome began asking online and aggregating the stories of *thousands* of others since 2010 who had the very same recollections. This solitary occurrence lead to Broome naming it: the Mandela Effect. But the effect wouldn't be constrained to this one event. As the stories online gained traction, an ever expanding litany of such shared (seemingly false) memories has continually been growing. Many famous examples include different spellings of popular brand names that people remember as one spelling, but upon inspection, they were always another spelling.

And though those kinds of instances aren't the most compelling evidence for what may be echoes of a simulation (or time reconstruction), there are others that seem more akin to the Mandela example itself. One such example is the position the hand of a famous sculpture — Auguste Rodin's "The Thinker" — is in. In your memory, where do you think his hand is resting? Many people (myself included) remember it as resting against his forehead. As it turns out, it's resting under his chin. Interestingly a photo exists of Irish playwright George Bernard Shaw, a friend of Rodin's, in the pose of The Thinker at a display for its unveiling. In that photo Shaw's hand is on his forehead. Another more disturbing historical example is of the man at Tiananmen square. As much as the Chinese government would like to pretend this incident never happened, it was in fact world wide news in 1989, and an emblem of its time. In what would be known as the Tiananmen square massacre, video footage of a solitary man carrying grocery bags stood in front of a line of tanks headed to enforce military might upon a citizen's revolt at the square. The tank would move, and so would the man to block it. After a few movements the tank stopped altogether as it was obvious the man was willing to die before clearing the way. Many people, as it turns out, have another memory of this incident that showed the man *actually* being run over! And in gruesome detail. One such person recalls the sight of blood on the ground after the tank ran him down as burned in her memory.

Perhaps the most compelling example, if not for its shock then for its extent within the world's population, is one from the Christian Bible itself. Many people recall hearing or learning bible verses that speak of how the lion will lay down with the lamb. And, although this imagery almost appears in two separate places in Isaiah, it's not quite right.

In Isaiah 11:6 it says,

> *"The wolf also shall dwell with the lamb, and the leopard shall lie down with the kid; and the calf and the young lion and the fatling together; and a little child shall lead them.". And again in Isaiah 65:25, "The wolf and the lamb shall feed together, and the lion shall eat straw like the bullock: and dust shall be the serpent's meat. They shall not hurt nor destroy in all my holy mountain, saith the LORD.".*

> — ISAIAH 11:6

Some parishioners are *so* certain that this imagery is wrong and that it used to be "the lion will lay down with the lamb" (signifying dual imagery of the Christ) that they believe their own childhood bibles have been altered. Many paintings can be found today that present the scene of the lion laying down with the lamb as well.

And while many of these instances may seem hard to understand through the lens of some necessary change in a simulated universe, our inability to understand each case as such doesn't negate the logic in the proposal itself. Many of us have heard of Chaos Theory. The idea that through an endless string of causality, the beating of a butterfly's wings in Japan could lead to a hurricane half way around the world. The lesson being to never underestimate a causal action due to its seeming insignificance. In fact, the idea that we cannot track all relevant causality should clearly leave latitude for grand ideas to be had and considered. Were it not for the internet the Mandela effect wouldn't have likely even been recognized or become a civilizational phenomenon. What else may be found in such ways?

Perhaps one of the reasons that mainstream science is apt to dismiss any form of simulation hypothesis (no matter if even at the cutting edge of quantum physics it's possibility resounds) is perhaps where it logically leads. For as one considers the idea that our existence is a fabrication, that idea itself presupposes the existence of a fabricator. Since the wide spread adoption of Charles Darwin's theory of Evolution in the early 1800s, science has been enjoying a respite from the ages preceding it that demanded the existence of a creator. No matter the theological school, every religion has its deities. And every religion has its own version of universal creation due to them. In an unceremonious and circuitous manner, simulation hypothesis brings science all the way back around to the possibility that someone or something created our universe and that very specific and important logic they created inherently governs it.

In the next and final chapter on simulation hypotheses, we're going to go back in time and beliefs to explore what it was that many religious and mystical practices had to say about the possibility that our reality is realistically a fabricated construct.

METAPHYSICAL SIMULATION

"After the conversations about Indian philosophy, some of the ideas of Quantum Physics that had seemed so crazy suddenly made much more sense."

— WERNER HEISENBERG

Between our exploration into consciousness, the unraveling of our perceived and recorded presumptions of existence and the seemingly unworldly realm of the quantum, there appears to me to be an enormous amount of what our total reality is that's missing from any given framework. With that consideration, one should be more apt to give credence to frameworks of the past that have reported their own explorations.

For, if we allow the humility to accept that we don't know much of anything (even given everything we know), then perhaps there's some of the everything we don't know that's been uncovered by those with a different viewpoint than our own.

As we set out in this chapter to explore reality from outside the vantage point of the scientific, allow yourself to set certain preconceptions aside and permit the metaphysical to make its case outside the pretext of what can be known or tested.

As we attempt (as Deleuze proposed) to "palpate the unknowable", assume the lens of one of the great stoic philosophers Socrates when he said of himself, "I know only one thing: that I know nothing.".

For millennia before the advent of computer technology many human thinkers have mused over the universe and the reality that they perceived within it. It's a natural, logical order of thought to wonder deeply about all of the questions and considerations we've already covered in this book thus far. What's most fascinating about looking back into the beliefs and worldviews that have sprung up from these efforts is how much they actually resemble many of the proposals and conclusions that modernity has come to by way of technological enhancement. It's not that they are the same, but that's not the point. The fascination lies not in their differences but in their similarities.

Perhaps when considering the similarities of both consciousness and reality, the most curiously comparable of the ancient traditions is that of the eastern religions. The oldest of which being Hinduism, thought by many scholars to be the world's oldest religion dating back over 4000 years. Among the eastern religions, Hinduism can be considered to be the seed that many of the others sprung forth from including Sikhism and Buddhism. In fact, Hinduism itself doesn't even consider itself one religion. It's considered a family of religions, each with their own deities, yet harmonious as a whole. When you look into any religion there can be a pretty direct and obvious bifurcation between each belief's mystical and philosophical (or metaphysical) traditions.To begin with we're going to focus on the philosophical and metaphysical traditions of belief, as therein lay many of the similarities alluded to earlier. And when exploring the metaphysics of Hinduism you cannot but be struck by the thought that they've been talking about a version of simulated reality for thousands of years before we had the technology to propose something like Niklas Boström has recently. When I first began learning about the metaphysical beliefs of the Hindus, I was pointed to a lecture by renowned twentieth century writer and self-styled philosopher, Alan Watts. In it he begins with a thought experiment. If you had the ability to dream anything you wanted to (without the constraints of time) where you could fit seventy-five years worth of experience in a single dream, what would you do? Most people would begin by fulfilling their every desire to the utmost degree. But after enough iterations of such utopias, anyone (like any of the wealthiest people in history) would inevitably grow bored of the ease of it all. Perhaps after that point you would begin adding challenge and difficulty to your dream scenario, making it more interesting to dream. Though at some point thereafter you may realize that even with challenge and difficulty, it's not a real challenge if you realize that it's a dream and you're controlling it. This leads to the logical conclusion that the most fulfilling way to enjoy your ability to dream anything that you'd like, would not only be to create a reality with challenge and difficulty built into it but to *forget* that you're the one who built the reality once you enter it.

In the Upanishads, the basic texts of Hinduism, one of them starts out by saying "In the beginning was the self. And looking around, it said, 'I am'.". This concept and thought experiment sums up (in a sense) much of the Hindu view of reality and consciousness into a version of what is philosophically termed cosmopsychism. This is the idea that the entire universe is conscious and that it all shares the same consciousness together. Considering Watt's dream thought experiment, in that paradigm it becomes self evident that not only is everything consciousness but it's all the same consciousness that's unconsciously experiencing itself!

Cosmopsychism was one of the paradigms I had not delved into in the first nine chapters. Focusing more on dualism to make the point of a distinction between the physical and the conscious, we'll now come back to exploring it for the sake of the reality conversation. Fascinating avenues open up and branch off when venturing down this idea stream.

Ideas about individualism and collectivism are some of the first. For example (from the view of individualism) if we were to presume the universe is but a play being both projected from and acted out by one all-encompassing consciousness, then are *we* that sole consciousness as the individual? That is to say, am *I* the only viewpoint within the dream, while everyone and everything else is a derivative projection of the same mind but unpossessed by it? Or (from the view point of collectivism) does a cosmopsychic consciousness embody everyone and everything regardless of any individual separation within the dream?

In the case of the first (individualistic) consideration, I feel a certain degree of trepidation. Without being able to prove for one or the other (as is the case for every metaphysical idea that we'll explore here), the idea of being the only entity of import within the entire system reeks of a narcissistic and dangerously nihilistic worldview to assume. In the sense that nothing beyond yourself as the individual truly matters, as it's all just a projection of the self, for the self and by the self.

To transpose this idea back into the paradigm of a digital simulation (you'll begin to see many of the aforementioned parallels when you do) it would presume the contextual difference between the "player one" avatar versus a "non-player character"(NPC) that all other beings in this paradigm would be presumed as. Although it's true, in the same way that we can only truly *know* that our own consciousness is conscious (recall the catch twenty-two of trying to discern if an AI were sentient or not) we can only empathetically presuppose consciousness into those around us. But I consider the possible folly of this being wrong and believing it right far worse than presuming it wrong and it being right in comparison. That is to say, living life as if you are player one in a world of NPCs holds more moral peril if that were not the case than living as if we are all equally conscious would, if in fact, everyone else turned out to be NPCs.

As for the second consideration (collectivism), this is more typically what is believed in a variety of manners within the Hindu family of religions. And it can present itself in more than one sense. For example, most of us even in the western world are broadly aware of the idea of reincarnation. How, when one dies, their soul or Atman (in Sanskrit meaning "self" or "breath") is transmigrated from their former body into a new one. What kind of body (human, animal or even insect) depends on the way you had spent your life previously, weighing the good versus the bad; the concept of Karma. Well if you were to consider the dream, or simulation, or grand play that is unconsciously acting out all of reality within itself, each life experience passes from one construct or avatar within that system to another to play that next role out. And while each individual viewpoint experiences itself and it's life as intrinsic to itself, the whole of the system is but one consciousness within itself, simultaneously living out all experiences throughout time.

This paradigm solves for a few mundane considerations about the arithmetic of reincarnation. The fact that there are ever more life forms tomorrow than there were the day before. Without understanding the entire system as a whole within itself, it would appear a contradiction to have more bodies than Atman to fill them. And besides the fact that there would be a limitless amount of vectors the One self could experience its grand play from, this entire construct could also, theoretically, suspend the necessity for time. And why would that matter? If the One self was unaware of its drama it had enacted would it be aware enough in that state to jump through the timeline of the play or would it be constrained by a linear path throughout it?

An interesting (albeit, not overtly Hindu) essay by author Andy Weir, titled *The Egg*, covers a version of this consideration in an unique and holistic way. In the essay two figures meet each other in the afterlife, or some way-station approximation of it. The one had just died while the other helped to explain to him what had happened and what will happen next. Through a series of back and forth questions the newly dead man finds out that he is to be sent back to earth but into a different body. As the two get to know each other further it's revealed that the man who's been at the way-station has been waiting for and guiding the newly dead man every time his most recent body died for some time. When this sage guide informs the man who he will embody next he's shocked to hear that it will be a Chinese peasant girl from the year 540 AD. As the sage would elaborate, not only could he be and *has* he been sent back and forth throughout time, but that *every* single person in all of human history will be or already was him! From Jesus to Hitler, from a middle aged family man to a middle ages peasant girl. All human experience has or will be his individual experience and that this entire process was, essentially, the *egg* that will prepare him (once all lives had been lived) to be brought into reality from.

The similarities from *The Egg* and the Hindu framework are, of course, very apparent. In fact I would be surprised if Weir didn't draw heavily from it or another belief system within the family of Hindu religions. The major take-away I drew from the essay though was that of empathy. Where not only should one morally consider others to be conscious as you are conscious but that they (in this story) literally were or would be *you*. And if we could only truly know that we ourselves were conscious, then in this paradigm, we ourselves were in fact everyone at all times!

But if we stray now away from the eastern theologies (and I know there were more we didn't cover like Taoism and

Confucianism) what of the western Abrahamic traditions speak to the idea of a simulation? Between Christianity and Islam, those two belief systems hold the top two spots for most followed religions on earth. But whether it's them, Judaism, or any of their subsects very little similarity exists between the eastern mystic religions and the Abrahamic ones. Well, in the details at least.

This is, in fact, a distinction that Christian theologians distinguish in the terminology of apophatic and cataphatic doctrines or language. Where apophatic (negative or distictive) considerations within the texts refer to concepts of difference or distinction (for example, the differences between God and man), cataphatic (positive or inclusive) concepts point to the similarities between the material and the divine. Another way of thinking about the two would be apophatic concepts are the more understandable or literal truths, while cataphatic would be the more mythological or image based concepts meant to resolve the unknowable aspects of the divine into an analog that is more readily understandable.

And (focusing on the mythological this time) it's in the more cataphatic texts and concepts that similarities regarding reality begin to show through once more. And although, unlike the Hindu beliefs of an single consciousness experiencing itself through all things, the Abrahamic canons believe in a single God as the divine creator of all things. And though they don't believe that all people are essentially the same consciousness within itself, they do believe that the breath of the One, omnipresent (everywhere at once) God resides within all people since the first man. Alan Watts also made an interesting comparison between Jesus (who was God come down to earth in physical form and, in so doing, abandoning his omnipotence [absolute power]) and the dreamer construct of the one consciousness entering its own internal creation to become subject to it.

Of course, as was alluded to in the last chapter, one thing that simulation hypothesis and the simulated multiverse hypothesis have in common with most of theology is that of a necessary creator or architect. This has primarily been the de facto assumption built into most all metaphysical world-views throughout time and culture. Besides the fact that ardent materialists see this as a cop out that doesn't require a rigorous investigation to back it up, the issue they will most often raise is that of a "chicken & egg" paradox. If our reality was built by a creator, who built the creator? This is routinely cited as a prima facie non-starter used to discount these kinds of metaphysical frameworks as fallacious. But it's my personal contention that there is a fallacy in such presumptions. Besides the point that even the big bang (meant to explain the emergence of the material universe) is itself another form of chicken & egg paradox, I'm going to take this opportunity to uncharacteristically interject my own personal suppositions as they stand at the time of writing. And though I don't propose them as any form of holistic framework, or even a solid explanation, the point here is to add more possibility to the realm of what actual reality *may* be.

When I say I see a fallacy in the issues taken against constructs that require a creator, the explanation of what I mean will apply not only to material reductionistic worldviews but also to the most common forms of simulation hypotheses as we have been exploring previously. And though none of these issues or opposing views can be proven (nor do they strictly disprove either of the above frameworks), that's not the point. My goal in this exploration is yet another widening of the possible parameters of the total reality outside of our perception.

Open and Closed Systems

There is a mechanical premise, when observing a machine, that speaks to an important difference between two kinds of systems. They are a closed versus an open system.

In a closed system all of the mechanisms of action (including their necessary energy sources) are contained within a single, holistic system. Everything the system and all its internal constituents requires to operate exists within the system. Nothing is required externally for the sake of the system. In contrast, an open system is one that not only can have external processes and energies added or subtracted to them by way of interaction with other such systems, but often time require such externalities for the sake of the system.

When the material universe is considered within a scientific pretense it's generally done so under the presumption that it's a closed system. That everything they find out about it must necessarily be constituent to its system and no externalities are considered to be outside of it, let alone vital to its existence. This isn't the lens that I personally use when considering the universe.

Like most enormous and enigmatic ideas, the best way I've found to attempt to describe them comes by way of analogy. So it's through analogy that I'll explain how I look at our reality and in what way I'd consider it to more aptly be defined as an open system than a closed one.

No matter what name, deity or construct you consider a prime architect to be that built the reality we inhabit, it appears to me a matter of logic that they wouldn't be subject to their creation. And setting aside the Hindu considerations from earlier (that such a deity would willingly subject themselves to their creation), at least at the inception of this reality, they, to an important degree, are distinct from it and the laws that govern it. It's with this idea in mind I propose the analogy of a terrarium. Without stretching the analogy too thin, if you were to construct a terrarium to house animals within, complete with all the trappings of a self contained environment, you as the creator of it wouldn't be subject to what happens within it. Moreover you could interact with its inhabitants at will and by necessity without having to become subject to its internal construct personally. In a broader interpretation of this imagery, if you could build within its walls laws that govern the inhabitants for their sake, why should you (being external to and hierarchically above it) be affected by the laws of the terrarium you built?

If you picture our universe as the terrarium, complete with the physical laws that govern it, things like gravity, causality and even time may not be limiting factors to an architect intelligence. It's this particular consideration, if true, that leads me to see things like the chicken and egg paradox and even a computational based superstructure to the universe as (for lack of a better descriptor) an error of limited imagination.

In the case of the "who created the creator" critique, who's to say they would even need to be created? So much of our expectations upon the ethereal are a projection of our own limitations. If causality is only a function of the terrarium (with its mass, its entropy and its derivative physical consequences), a master architect wouldn't need a predecessor. Nor should it be constrained to the effects of linear time. As Einstein illuminated, time is a function of the forth dimension (spacetime) upon mass. It can be slowed down by extreme speeds, it can be sped up by gravitational waves, and it can be flipped upside down at the quantum level via retrocausality. Just because *we* can't escape its flow why should that constraint be projected upon anything outside of or supersedent to the terrarium we're subject within?

In a similar way, I do in fact consider our reality to be some form of simulation. But, not in the computer sense. To me, again, it feels that we are projecting our own constraints and logic (though important within our universe to us) upon something we may have absolutely no reference point to begin to qualify in regards to necessary governing parameters. So, in that way, I see an argument that begins with computer logic (being rooted in familiar architecture at the level of modern humans) as unnecessarily narrow. And though it makes logical sense that beyond the crossing of the uncanny valley, humanity could build a simulation that theoretically suggests we're also in one, this too could be too logical at our level to translate in any meaningful, transcendent way. It, for one, brings back the chicken and egg paradox. But, beyond that, there are at least two metaphysical considerations that would confound that concept's functionality.

Firstly, if we once again call back to Gilles Deleuze's observation about time in the present, remember how he made the point that there is no discrete measure of the present moment. And how, he suggested, that the present (which is all we ever experience) is more likely the exact intersection of the past and the future. Try (as best you can) to view time as its own sort of terrarium. Something that could be crafted and affected outside the confines of its affect on the craftsman. Like two massive venn diagrams, of past and future, that barely connect at one point of their periphery. And it's only at that epicenter that our causal universe (as far as our present interpretation of it) exists. From our vantage point, trapped at that intersection, it doesn't even make sense how anything existing outside of it could plausibly *do* anything. As every one of our actions are clocked in linear time. But, I leave open the possibility that our universe— time and all — could be an open system, affected by something entirely unencumbered by all of the specifics of our existence. This would make any inevitable computer simulation, from the first iteration on, no more important or different within the total terrarium than any other point of time that could be experienced.

This leads to the second confounding consideration, that of consciousness as the qualifying variable of experience. If on one hand we were matrix styled avatars whose consciousness was ported into our bodies from a base level physical reality, is our consciousness part of us at all? That is to say, of the base level entity whose consciousness is being ported into us unknowingly, is that consciousness in them or in us? Can it be equally in both bodies at the same time? What if we (in the second level simulated reality) build and project our consciousness (which is still being ported into us from the base level) into another avatar? Is the same consciousness being multiplied or is it being moved from one embodiment to another *ad infinitum*? I'm not opposed to the idea of certain separations of the duality of consciousness from body (whether by means of astral projection like in chapter seven or even losing time by way of being choked or knocked unconscious [which falls more under the category of an interruption between radio and signal]) but a porting of consciousness in the multiplicitous manner suggested above seems a stretch.

But if consciousness could not be ported in the matrix sense more than once, the best we could create, so far as a computational tower is concerned, would be one level. So that any additional simulations birthed within that first level simulation wasn't its own simulation but just a facet of the first one. For example if a base level being stepped into a simulation level avatar and that avatar stepped into a simulation within that simulation, the experience of the "third level" reality would still be happening in the second level reality. The base level may *think* it's in the third layer but the third layer is just a figment within the second. So that in essence, the consciousness of the base level is only ever in one possible layer of reality removed from the prime reality. And in that case I don't see a difference between the terrarium construct if the prime architect outside of the terrarium was what we consider consciousness as a whole.

And that would lead us full circle once more, back to where we have to wonder what our consciousness even is. And if we and reality are the product of a grand intelligence, is consciousness a feature of the terrarium they built or a feature of them themselves? Calling back to the Hindu sole consciousness experiencing itself or the Abrahamic One God who breathed himself into man.

If the system we're in is an open one perhaps the animating, experiential aspect of it comes externally in from the outside. Unifying the ideas of consciousness as exogenous to, yet entangled with the human body, and a form of first level simulation from the vantage point of the prime architect that our animating experience (within our universe) follows from.

In the third and final section of the reality portion of this book a long considered and widely debated question will be explored. Because if we only perceive a narrow band of total reality, what other affecting aspects of it exist that can effect us in it? Or, more to the point, that *we* can affect to our benefit?

SECTION 3: MALLEABILITY

TESLA'S UNIVERSAL KEY

"To understand the Universe, you must understand the language in which it's written, the language of Mathematics."

— GALILEO GALILEI

I f, being trapped at the intersection of past and future, we find ourselves vastly unable to do more than observe the functionality of our terrarium, to what degree if any, do we have by way of adjusting its parameters?

Man is, if anything, a creator. We've mastered, manipulated and subdued the natural world between the power of our curiosity multiplied by our opposable thumbs. Is it possible to also manipulate our reality? Many have tried over the ages, and some make claims to these ends.

In the final three chapters of our delve into reality, we'll explore what avenues can lead people to believe they can hack the fabric of what is real.

Between all of the different views, beliefs and pronouncements about reality up until this chapter, no matter which (if any) changed your idea of what existence is, they should at least have opened up new branching networks of possibility to it all.

Whether it's a self contained simulation built atop another, a nanoscopic sub-realm that runs counter to all known physics, or a dream that we're unwittingly living out; all of these hold a plausible key to how we can hack our level of reality.

Like Neo, in *The Matrix*, attempting to bend a spoon with his mind simply by the realization that there *is* no spoon — is it possible to locate these kinds of loopholes or shortcuts in reality to affect the impossible? Before we explore one school of thought who believes they can, we need to lay some ground work by examining the claims of a certified super genius from the 1800s.

The Mysterious Nikola Tesla

In the year 1856, a child was born to Serbian parents in what is now currently Croatia. This boy, unbeknownst to his parents (a priest for a father and a mother of deep familial roots in Serbia), would wind up changing the course of humanity world wide by the age of thirty years old.

Nikola Tesla was a super genius by any standard. Born with a rare and important mental trait called an eidetic memory. Stories of his capacity to recall information exactly as he remembered it were common among those who knew him. Beyond the power of vivid recollection, his ability to picture complex mechanisms in his mind and bring them into reality was astounding even within the rarified company of elite engineers he would later join the ranks of. Between his cognitive advantages and a natural propensity to reexplore settled subjects (these days called "first principles" thinking) Tesla was a star pupil by the age of nineteen in the electrical engineering program at the Imperial-Royal Technical College in Graz, Austria.

What would ensue in the proceeding years (upon his arrival in the United States in 1884) was a battle of the ages when it came to the cultural application of publicly available electricity world wide. Tesla would both work with and then stand opposed to famous inventor of the incandescent light bulb and head of General Electric — Thomas Edison. The battle between these two great visionaries revolved primarily around the conceptual and practical applications of Edison's direct current (DC) energy and Tesla's alternating current (AC) energy. A bitter and sordid rivalry would flare between the business savvy Edison and the superior engineering vision of Tesla.

And *vision* is the correct term to use. Because on top of his intellectual merits, Nikola Tesla had several peculiar and idiosyncratic quirks. One in particular was that of literal visions that would strike him uncontrollably. One such occurrence happened during the height of his feud with Edison. He was fighting a severe headache which prompted him to leave his apartment and walk outside for fresh air. During this walk, as the story goes, he felt a shock of pain and a flash of light that brought him to his knees. In that moment he saw a vivid vision, in all its mechanical intricacies, of the design for an AC motor that harnessed electromagnetism using alternating current to produce electricity. This he would use to bring the induction motor (used in hydroelectric power generation) into reality.

This form of spontaneous epiphany is one of the more enigmatic character- istics about Tesla that many present day academics don't like to lend credence to. And if all that came out of them were ideas with no function then they would have been easier to write off as the insane conjuring of a mentally ill thinker. But between this motor and other such instances, credence (at the very least) is due. In fact, there are many other more inauspicious idiosyncrasies Tesla had that make it easier to discount some of his less causally demonstrable proclamations (one of which being the core purpose of this chapter). He exhibited many quirks that spoke more to psychiatric disorders than one likes to have in their super geniuses. Like the affinity he had for pigeons, and not just at the level of fascination. He spoke of an infatuation he had for certain pigeons like "a man has for a woman".

Tesla also had a peculiar compulsion with certain numbers that bordered on obsessive compulsive disorder. And it's at this point where he presents perhaps his most cryptic and otherworldly pronouncement. As we explore this area of his insights (before casting judgment upon perhaps one of the greatest outside the box thinkers in modern history) consider the following from Socrates, "The greatest blessings granted to mankind come by way of madness, which is a divine gift.". Between the fantastic yet functional visions and the inexplicable obsessions and proclivities of Nikola Tesla, I'm certain Socrates would see in him that divine gift of madness. It's what Tesla wrote, regarding a certain set of numbers, that people all the way up to the present day believe that in them lies a universal hack to our reality.

The number set is as simple as it is puzzling. Three, six and nine. This, without much more to go on, is what prompted Tesla to write, "If you only knew the magnificence of the 3, 6 and 9, then you would have the key to the universe.".

That's quite a statement for a man of his intellect to make. But he believed it, fully. So much so that he structured his life in extreme ways to coordinate with these numbers. For instance, he would only stay in a hotel room with a number that was divisible by three. When doing the dishes, he would use eighteen dish cloths as this number divides by three, six, and nine. He would even circle the block of a building he meant to enter three times before crossing its threshold. Many people look at these odd behaviors as emblematic of psychosis. But to Tesla, it was critically important that he do whatever he could to add to the primacy of those numbers within his life.

This idea has carried on with those who follow his example up into modernity on the presumption that whatever it was that Tesla saw in these simple integers (enough to confidently assert them to be the keys to the universe) can unlock the code of existence. In fact, it's within existence that those who ascribe to its importance see these numbers appearing from top to bottom. Especially that of the triplet or trinity that appear in everything from mathematics, to nature, to history and culture. Be it at the atomic level existing in three base constituents of electron, proton and neutron, or the trinity of matter in solid, liquid and gas. One very odd place that the adherents of this methodological search for Tesla's keys of the universe venture is into mathematics. And, specifically, as it pertains to an irregular application of logic called a "digital root".

The concept of the digital root is actually quite simple. You can take any number, no mater how large, and add its digits together until you come to a single digit between one and nine. For example, if you would take the random number of 27,492, to find its digital root, you would find the sum of 2+7+4+9+2 which equals 24. Since 24 is still two digits, you simply repeat the process until you only have one digit. In the case of 24, it's 2+4=6. Therefore the digital root of 27,492 is 6.

Tesla code maximalists will present an infinite repeating equation that will have you double the product of the most recent doubling starting with

1. This sequence looks like:

$1 = 2$
$2 = 4$
$4 = 8$
$8 = 16$
$16 = 32$
$32 = 64$
$64 = 128$ and so on ad infinitum.

When you devolve all of these products down to their digital roots in order, you'll be presented with a repeating pattern of 2, 4, 8, 7, 1. Notice anything about that pattern? More to the point, notice anything missing? The numbers 3, 6 and 9 will never appear. Strange, sure. But what if you halved numbers starting at 1? It will look like this:

1
.5
.25
.125
.0625
.03125

Resolving these through the same digital root equation sequence once again presents with and infinitely repeating pattern of 1, 5, 7, 8, 4, 2. Notice again, the lack of 3, 6 and 9.

Ok, that's twice as strange as the first time. But the Tesla code seekers aren't done there. They would now have you start from the number 3 instead and double it into infinity, *or* half it into infinity. Doing so you'll find that the digital roots of those products are only ever a repeating pattern of 3 and 6. Moreover, the exact same thing happens when you double or half starting from 6 instead of 3. Again you'll get 3 and 6 as the repeating pattern of all their digital roots.

But what about 9 then? This number doesn't disappoint those who may be holding their breath. Running the very same experiment, either doubling or halving starting from 9, will only ever present a digital root of 9s. Nothing but 9s, all the ways up and all the way down.

Now I'll admit, upon seeing this, I found it oddly compelling at the least. Certainly strange enough to catch my interest. I searched out other explanations for such an occurrence. Finding patterns in math isn't unheard of. In fact, math itself is somewhat of an exercise in pattern detection, broadly speaking. And, as it turns out (without getting too deep), there's a geometric function in math that has to do with the multiplier (in this case, 2, 3, 6 and 9) as it opposes a modulus number. Using this pattern producing formula, the repetitive sequences from before seem derivative only to base 10. If you changed the base to another number, similar (but less exciting) patterns form that don't account for the special considerations of 3, 6 and 9.

What they do start to present, the further you expand the multiplier and modulus, is an important and powerful geometric pattern called a cardioid. The cardioid (among other places it appears in geometric math) is one of the resounding features seen prominently in the Mandelbrot Set fractal mentioned in chapter thirteen.

So, where does this leave the universal key? Well, even when the shocking numerical patterns from before have been logically demystified, there are a few odd places the number 9 still shows up. Like the digital roots of:

> The speed of light: 186282 m/sec 1+8+6+2+8+2=27
> 2+7= 9
> Diameter of the earth: 7920 miles 7+9+2+0=18
> 1+8= 9
> Diameter of the Sun: 864000 miles 8+6+4+0+0+0=18
> 1+8= 9
> Diameter of the Moon: 2160 miles 2+1+6+0= 9

With the consideration of there only being nine single digit integers, the fact is, every digital root (no matter where the number came from) has a 1 in 3 chance of being either a 3, 6 or 9. So it shouldn't be too surprising (when you seek them) that they will pop up all over the place.

It becomes harder and harder to justify the metaphysics of this kind of patterning the more it gets unraveled. But was this even what Tesla was alluding to with his cryptic proclamation about them being the key to the universe? Remember he never explained what he meant by that, and it's been left up to subjectivity in the proceeding years since.

But if these digital root suggestions are not the universal key that Tesla spoke of, what was it that he saw in those numbers? The man responsible for alternating current, radio waves, hydroelectric power, x-rays and more *so* believed in their universal importance that he structured his personal life around them in a radical way. Perhaps that is where the key is to be found — in personal applications. Recently, many people have been attempting to apply the numbers directly to their lives in a similar but different way than Tesla did. And they claim some fascinating results for their efforts.

In the next chapter we're going to start by looking at these applications and find out if there is something about the way they're being used that actually *does* affect our reality in a way that could be seen as a tapping into the universe around us.

VIBRATIONAL UNIVERSE

"If you want to understand the universe think in terms of energy, frequency and vibration."

— NIKOLA TESLA

I t's interesting to see that the more you look into reality from a modern view point, the more the similarities merge between view points from the distant past.

We saw that happen quite clearly in chapter fifteen between Hinduism and quantum physics in regards to a metaphysical and virtual simulation.

There's another similarity where the quantum and the theological intersect. And it's at this intersection that those working to inject Tesla's numbers into their lives may in fact be tapping into something beneath the surface of our perception in their efforts.

***

In the most recent iteration of a search for Nikola Tesla's 3, 6, 9 universal key, a couple of pathways crossed. The exploration for their primacy in mathematics continues. Meanwhile what people have been doing with them personally and practically is quite interesting, and they may be wandering into a reality hack of their own.

Over the pandemic years of 2020 through 2022, a trend took hold on certain social platforms. This trend centered around Tesla's numbers in a way totally peripheral to the proposed importance they have in nature, history or math. Many different people took many different approaches to the same application, and that was to use some form of 3, 6, and 9 in a metaphysical practice called manifestation.

Manifestation became a cultural phenomenon around a film turned book called *The Secret* that released in 2006. In *The Secret* an ancient idea was re- branded into a concept it coined "The law of attraction". To sum up its thesis, everything in the universe is vibrational. If you can match or harmonize your vibrations with the things that you desire in your life, you will attract them to you. Thus, the law of attraction. Clearly, in the scientific sense, that isn't a law by actual definition. But in a colloquial sense, it's presumed a principal of practice at least.

Now lets explore this claim more deeply. Because proponents on this practice are quite certain of its validity. Enough so for any curious person to take notice. In fact, it was for this reason (I believe) that people began plugging in Tesla's numbers and subsequently saw results.

So, what is it that people are practically doing in efforts to manifest their desires into reality around them? To be honest, it's a very simple practice that really doesn't seem to have a "correct" method of application. More or less, through means of writing, meditating, visualizing or verbalizing their desires, a person more and more attunes themselves (at a material, vibrational level) to those things they focus their attentions on. In the case of the Tesla numbers, people were writing down their sole desire they wanted to see manifested in their life three times in the morning, six times at noon, and nine times in the evening.

As far as a necessity of input for desired outcome is concerned, that's not a very large requirement. But does it work? And if so, why? These are the important questions to explore and discover, on the chance that there's actual validity in this practice. Because, if there is, this may in fact be a utilitarian method of manipulating reality for our benefit.

The Physical

One of the first contentions to arise from people skeptical of manifestation techniques revolves around a common false positive that happens when someone is seeking a certain result. What's more, it turns out that you don't even need to be consciously seeking the result to find it.

If you've ever had the experience of buying a new vehicle and then suddenly noticing them everywhere you go, this is the kind of false positive in question. What's interesting is that we understand, biologically, why that is, and it all revolves around a fascinating and hyper-valuable portion of the brain called the reticular activating system (RAS).

The RAS portion of the brain is a small section near the brain stem that's about the size of your pinkie finger. Four out of your five major senses (excluding only smell) require the qualification of their information through this area. It's for that reason that the RAS is referred to as the "gatekeeper" of the brain. For anything to be considered important information (as received through sight, sound, taste or touch), the RAS is where that qualifying function occurs. Valuable tasks like cardiovascular function, pain perception, circadian cycle, fight or flight response, our ability to focus, and our subconscious ability to filter what is relevant in our environment to build our perception of reality are rooted here.

The important part of that insight is the *subconscious* part. Our brains, as the epicenter of our senses, take in billions of bits worth of information every day. It's so flooded by input that the subconscious work (like the RAS's filtering function) that's going on in the background actually accounts for as much as 95% of our brain activity. Included in that percentage are other functions you wouldn't want to be consciously responsible for, like breathing, blinking, pumping blood or digesting food. But it's within this busy work (especially that of the RAS) that our perception of reality springs forth. Though it serves many important purposes (like being able to hear your name called in a noisy room), it can only do so via the exclusion of most of the information your senses are perceiving at any given moment.

Therefore, it's by dint of this biological functionality that some people who are critical towards manifestation as a superstitious endeavor say that all you're doing is reattuning your RAS to seek out your desires; not to draw them to you.

Interestingly, some advocates of manifesting look at the very same contention and consider it the exact reality hack in question. In a similar sense to the placebo effect — how the mind can affect the body when it thinks it's been given healing medicine when it hasn't — by adjusting the RAS to filter for the means to attain your desires, you'll find the path to them that you didn't know was there.

But, as true and beneficial as that may be, that's not exactly what is being proposed by the more metaphysical versions and beliefs of manifestation advocates. And so it's there that we really must dive into to try and find if manifesting is something even deeper than just a biological pattern filtering function.

Metaphysical

As was mentioned at the outset of this chapter, the statements regarding vibration are where the real base of the manifestation beliefs are rooted. And though there is science that will be added into the mix, where this idea started from is much more ancient and sacred knowledge than that.

Several eastern theologies and philosophies, for thousands of years, have incorporated versions of sacred or divine vibrations. Going back to the Hindu beliefs, there is a word or sound that is considered so fundamental and sacred to their beliefs that the symbol for it (like the cross to a Christian) is the very icon used to portray the faith. The symbol is written as � in Sanskrit and is spelled Om (pronounced *ohm*) in English. Among many of the Vedic texts, passages will both start and end with Om. One explanation (found in the Aitareya Brahmana) of why that is, speaks to the vibrational importance bestowed upon it. This Hindu text explains Om as "an acknowledgment, melodic confirmation, something that gives momentum and energy to a hymn". More to the point, Om is believed to be the vibrational representation and essence of the supreme consciousness, Brahman. The idea of synchronizing your intentions with the universe at the vibrational level is absolutely core to the belief.

But even at the core of reality, everything is vibrating. Because everything is energy. It's also a statement of fact to say this. If you were to pick up an inanimate rock that has no life and no ability to move itself; even that is composed of nothing but energy. Being that it consists of molecules, which consist of atoms, which consist of quanta which are quantifiable energy measured in waveforms and frequency — ie: vibrations. Literally all matter in the known universe is vibrating at all times. This leads to the question that many of the metaphysical belief systems address in some way, "do people emit and/or causally interact with the physical universe vibrationally?".

Remember back to our exploration into some of the stranger aspects of quantum mechanics. Einstein dubbed one of them "spooky action at a distance". This had to do with entanglement of quanta where you could separate entangled particles by any stretch of distance and watch in real time as an effect on one would present the same reaction in the other. As recognized as that is, no one knows how it works. Some people (breaking the first wall) note other such intangible spooky actions all the way up into the Newtonian level of reality. Things that often get labeled as a "sixth sense" or an unexplainable coincidence. There are instances where someone close to you has something terrible happen to them and you feel the need to call them. Or you get the undeniable sense that you're being watched even without seeing who it is. It's been a well documented occurrence world wide of some form of psychic connection between identical twins.

When, even a world apart, they can sense that something is wrong with their genetic duplicate. Whatever the method of interaction is (either between entangled quanta or human level existence), there seems as if some level of reality pervades below the surface of visual detection. Some substrate, like an invisible ocean of interconnectivity, allows for interaction between energetic forces in a way that defies distance and separation. Perhaps it is that throughout all levels of reality, energy (via frequency and vibration) is the currency of this substrate. As it stands today, such a substrate of reality is recognized even though we know virtually nothing about it. It accounts for almost all of the known universe, but we can't even figure out how to realistically research it. They call it dark matter and dark energy. For so far as tangible mass-energy is concerned (the matter we can see and interact with), this only accounts for 5% of the known universe. While dark matter (26.8%) and dark energy (68.2%) make up the other 95% of our reality. An apt analogy would be a piece of paper that's been written on. All we interpret is the writing on the page, but without the paper it's written on (which is the majority of what makes up the page), the ink wouldn't form the information we're reading.

Perhaps it is that these spooky phenomenon work through some layer of existence happening behind the scenes in that 95% we can't explore. And what people are witnessing through vibrational manifestation is a function of the connectivity through that universal substrate. It could literally be vibrational interaction, or it could be some other analogous force between like vectors.

What is happening when a child gets a sense for someone they've never met before? They're repelled by something about them unencumbered by objective visual cues. Or when a dog gets defensive of their owner around someone they've never met, to the exclusion of all the other other people in the room. Some beliefs would call it an aura, or an energy that's being sensed as it negatively interacts with your own. Conversely, how is it that certain people get along with each other and make fast friends before circumstances would logically dictate? Some people speak of soulmates, and not exclusively in a sexual relationship.

There seems to me to be a legitimate avenue of consideration that could more likely be tested through experience and practice than by typical scientific rigor. And it's due to this consideration that I'm not surprised to find those who spend active practice in some form of energetic projection would be able to hone in on accessing this substrate for what it's worth. Through meditation, through visualization, through specific journaling, through prayer or through positive affirmations. Each of these practical applications of expressing specific desires has been show for millennia to propagate what some might call luck and others call manifestation.

And even if, at the end of the day, all we're witness to is a trick of the reticular activating system that's leading us towards actuating our inner most desires — a placebo can still fix what ails you.

Though, I'm of the impression that there's far more going on than just fidgeting with our software. And in the final chapter on reality, we're going to look into an esoteric tradition (traced all the way back to the Greeks and Egyptians) whose principles claim to reveal how to navigate and manipulate reality, far beyond the material.

THE HERMETIC PRINCIPLES

"I regard consciousness as fundamental. I regard matter as derivative from consciousness."

— MAX PLANCK

F rom the physical to the immaterial, the literal to the mythological, we've walked many different paths in our journey through the concepts and constructs of reality. And while, surely, not all of them can be true, the truth (as it seems) may be less about what's perceived and more about what's believed than we ever realized.

But there is at least one more road in this branching network we've not tread upon yet. One that seems, perhaps, to connect many of the dots we've illuminated up until this point. What's more, it lays out reality for you like an instruction manual on how to use it. Complete with seven principles meant as your guide.

According to science, broadly speaking, our greatest task is to discover what is true and actionable. The causal mechanisms and immutable laws of governance that create the canvas of our universe.

We live in a society utterly created through and subsumed by the primacy of science. Our technologies and the civilizations they've enabled are the glory of our times. But before our times, science held a place within a trinity of pillars. Between these three laudable and interdependent beams— Philosophy, Theology and Science — past cultures have rested their many constructs.

Without taking away from the benefits a strong focus on science has afforded us, we've given it monolithic status to the derision of the other two pillars. Theology is repudiated as fantasy and philosophy as superfluous in the shadow of scientific rigor. But as we've seen throughout this book by now, there are simply parts (if not the majority) of reality that are inaccessible to science. And to wait for science to proclaim the truth about them is to await, at best, a false conclusion. So it is that much of one's exploration must necessarily expand outwardly into the realms of the philosophical and the theological to try and form those two pillars to rest a balanced worldview upon.

And of the many and varied structures that have been formed over human history, there's one specific and curious culmination that is as simple as it is perplexing. The roots of which are as mysterious as the knowledge it prescribes. But, of its guiding tenets, you may notice a particular similarity to many of the ideas postulated already in this book. This school of thought is called Hermeticism.

The Hermetic Lore

Hermeticism is nothing if not replete with mystery and lore. So it's important to give a certain amount of back story to its historic tradition before we open up into its core tenets.

The name itself is a direct homage to its founder, Hermes Trismegistus. He was a man thought to have lived in the first century A.D. He became widely known in both the Grecian and Egyptian cultures of the time for his great wisdom. Two highly regarded ancient texts — the Emerald Tablet and the Corpus Hermeticum — are attributed to him. In the traditions of his time he was considered to be a master of the universe and found his way into Greek mythology as Hermes and Egyptian mythology as Thoth. The tales of Hermes Trismegistus claimed he had lived for thousands of years and acquired his knowledge throughout that time.

After his time, the wisdom he passed on (that eventually became the Hermetic principles) was primarily transmitted by way of oral tradition and secret texts. Even the oral tradition was specifically a secretive tradition. It was, for centuries, considered highly valuable wisdom not to be shared by the masses. Though, at the turn of the 20th century, this would change.

In the year 1908, a book was published whose author (or authors) was simply dubbed "The Three Initiates". Many people propose it was authored by a man named William Walker Atkinson who lived and wrote in that time. The title of the book was *The Kybalion: A Study of the Hermetic Philosophy of Ancient Egypt and Greece*. This book is, essentially, a summarized, modern depiction of many more ancient Hermetic canonical beliefs before it. Though it's seen more as an introduction to a much denser body of knowledge, it's within these pages that the (now popularized) seven Hermetic principles are laid out and explained in detail. It's these principles that we will explore before closing off the reality portion of this book. Because there may within it exist functional hacks to cause reality to work for us.

The Seven Principles

Of the 170 or so pages of The Kybalion, for the purpose of this exploration, we'll simply run through each of the seven principles in order, with a quote from the Kybalion about it, and with some thoughts interjected thereafter.

The First Principle: The Principle of Mentalism. "The All is Mind; the Universe is Mental."

This, the first and foundational principle of Hermetic beliefs, is almost precisely what Alan Watts was describing about Hinduism through the dream thought experiment in chapter fifteen. Hemeticists believe that reality is consciousness and that everything is a mental projection of that universal "All" we're each a part of. Though they don't indicate a specific God, they believe that God *is* consciousness or thought itself, and that reality is a projection of the essence of God. Through that reasoning, they state that we have the capability to affect our reality through practices that focus on the mind's abilities of projection itself. For if God (who is all consciousness) is projecting this all, and we ourselves are conscious, then we also have this ability to some important degree.

The Second Principle: The Principle of Correspondence. "As above, so below; as below, so above."

This one is a commonly used colloquial phrase these days. It has a number of different uses and connotations in the Hermetic sense though. In one sense, it conveys a fractal similarity between all levels of reality. This is certainly seen throughout nature, all the way up and all the way down in many different ways. The term correspondence speaks to an interactivity between these levels that the Hermeticist sees as both important and actionable. For example, the insights of the first principle relate to the second in that if God is all consciousness and we are a consciousness within that, then we can affect reality as God has in the fractal sense. More specifically though, the Kybalion speaks to vibrational levels of existence that layer on top of each other. In the same way the cellular, molecular and atomic do on top of each. And that, in the vibrational sense, you can correspond between higher and lower levels based upon your understanding of them and subsequent actions that affect your relation to each.

The Third Principle: The Principle of Vibration. "Nothing rests; every- thing moves; everything vibrates."

Another thing that, ostensibly, is ancient knowledge that matches modern science. Every material thing is a form of energy which is a form of vibration. Beyond that, the Hermeticists state that not only do all material things vibrate, but every spiritual thing also has a unique vibrational frequency. In this way ideas like manifestation find a kindred philosophy. In an actionable sense, the goal would be to work at lifting yourself into a higher spiritual vibration, to both avoid the lower levels but also to bring yourself into alignment with the other higher level frequencies around you. If you were to picture each frequency as a horizontal layer, the higher you rise vertically, the more accessible the things at each layer become to you. In fact, in this idea, they would *only* be accessible to you if you were to reach their level of vibration.

The Fourth Principle: The Principle of Polarity. "Everything is dual; everything has poles; everything has its pair of opposites; like and unlike are the same; opposites are identical in nature but different in degree; extremes meet; all truths are but half-truths; all paradoxes may be reconciled."

This principle is a very old piece of knowledge that's also a deceptively deep philosophical truth. The Taoist concept of the yin and yang is another well recognized version of this fourth principle. It goes without saying that there is a diametric opposite to all things. Summer has winter, left has right, male has female, darkness has light. What Taoism presents is more than just the opposite nature of these things, but that each requires the other for balance. Too much of one over the other creates imbalance, chaos and destruction. But destruction in itself is one side of a whole that leads to eventual construction, leading back into unity and balance. The Hermeticists continue this philosophy in an interesting manner. They propose that both sides of the spectrum are, in fact, the same thing; "identical in nature but different in degree". The shadow is the same as the light. Though scientifically false, it's philosophically true. Total darkness is an absence of light, which means that a single photon of light in absolute darkness is technically lighter, but still dark. In this sense, it's clear that these total opposites are just either end of a single spectrum. The spectrum is the same thing, though the degrees are entirely different. Like two sides of the same coin, at the edges, both sides meet in a cyclical and infinite connection of pure opposites. Whether

Taoist, Hermeticist, or Stoic philosophy, this principle logically leads to a balancing of mind in regards to all things. It leads one not to react to an unwanted effect, knowing that it's just the necessary opposite in a union between poles that will meet, swing and repeat again for eternity. There's no need to wail for the night when you know the day will follow.

The Fifth Principle: The Principle of Rhythm. "Everything flows, out and in; everything has its tides; all things rise and fall; the pendulum-swing manifests in everything; the measure of the swing to the right is the measure of the swing to the left; rhythm compensates."

In the mechanical sense, this was a proven set of physical laws called the Laws of Motion as was written in the *Principia* in 1687 by Sir Issac Newton. Newton, himself a believer in Hermeticism, brought this idea of rhythm into the mathematical and scientific realms to reliably define what is witnessed in the physical world as energy acts upon mass. A pendulum is the perfect example of the Newtonian three laws of motion in action.

In the philosophical sense, Hermeticists extend this principle to all things material and immaterial. The actions of a civilization, the moods of an individual, both are affected by a perpetual and inevitable swing between poles. Those who follow this as a universal principle will not only weather the negative effects of a down swing in anticipation of the up swing, but will work to actively counter the down swings in their life with their opposite inertia however they can. Furthermore, knowing that an equal swing is due, they recognize the dangers of forcibly overloading either swing, as the next down swing will mirror its intensity. Though, it's believed that a master of the seven principles will have the ability to transcend duality in all ways, that's not how believers typically view themselves.

The Sixth Principle: The Principle of Cause and Effect. "Every cause has its effect; every effect has its cause; everything happens according to law; chance is but a name for law not recognized; there are many planes of causation, but nothing escapes the law."

Besides the obvious mechanical correlation of this and the laws of physics, this again extends to the ethereal beyond human level perceivable reality. In fact this principle rings of Sam Harris' Illusion of Free Will argument or the Descartes' Demon thought experiment. And though I hold my reservations in regards to the totality of this idea (as stated in chapters six and fifteen), at least within the physical, this is demonstrably true. Hermetics would contend that it remains true throughout all levels of reality; "chance is but a name for law not recognized". In my personal view (to call back to the terrarium analogy of chapter fifteen), were our reality an open system where certain causality could stem from outside of its whole *inwards*, the same may not (and likely *would* not) apply from the open system back upon that which is outside of it in kind.

And perhaps that's all that's being spoken to in this principle. Only that within our universal reality. Anything feasibly outside of it that could foist a cause inwards would be outside this principle's consideration.

The Seventh Principle: The Principle of Gender. "Gender is in everything; everything has its masculine and feminine principles; gender manifests on all planes."

In cultural times like those of the 2020s, gender is largely considered to be a social construct where hard lines blur and definitions become fully fluid. On the face of something like the seventh principle, ire may be garnered by those presuming it invalidates any such views. And though there is a certain rigidity to its implications, once fully understood, it applies to both firmly held views of gender as well as the spectrum that's largely being presented in modern sociology.

As with each of the preceding six principles, universality is assumed in this principle's application. Not just with sexual considerations, but in all things, "everything has its masculine and feminine principles". Viewing this with the addition of the principle of polarity, though there is an implicit duality, these opposites exist upon a single spectrum that all things find a place within. For example, a male could have several feminine qualities, as could a female have several masculine ones. In fact, it would be considered a matter of fact that all males present certain feminine qualities and vice versa. This is in line with, not against the seventh principle. But, beyond the human, feminine and masculine qualities are presumed present in all things as part of the vital balance of energies within the universe. In all vital as well as mundane activities there are masculine and feminine attributes. If you breath in you're using a masculine energy. When you breath out you're accessing the femininity of breath. Without an acknowledgment of their existence, imbalance is sure to arise where each is predominantly necessary.

Reality in Conclusion

Whether the lore behind Hermetics is true, the principles in the Kybalion it espouses are intriguingly copacetic with much of what has been explored in this portion on reality all throughout. And, as one builds up the three pillars of science, philosophy and theology within their own construct of what's real, it's within the similarities that we discover what we can about what reality is.

If anything, after a wide enough exploration of what we know, it should become exceptionally clear how *little* we know of total reality. It would be hubris to presume we know even one percent of everything there is to know. And in that view, with all humility, it becomes apparent that whatever anyone knows about reality is (at best) a proprietary montage patchwork of what little we know in total. So, it shouldn't be surprising when Gilles Deleuze says that truth is an act of creation. And that each and every person (just like the uniqueness of their AI created commercial social media avatars) has their own patchwork, built from bits and pieces of the less than one percent of what's known, that makes up what they call reality.

And as we close this second of three portions, don't feel as though the confusion and enormity of it all should dwarf your personal importance within the universe. In fact, quite the contrary, we are about to open up the final portion of this book and explore the very core of what it is to exist at all — our purpose.

PORTION III: PURPOSE

"The mystery of human existence lies not in just staying alive, but in finding something to live for."

—Fyodor Dostoevsky

SECTION 1: THE MIND OF THE ANT

19

DISCOVERING PURPOSE

"If you can't figure out your purpose, figure out your passion. For your passion will lead you right into your purpose."

— T.D. JAKES

It's perhaps one of the most timeless questions of all, "What is my purpose in life?". It's one that everyone will ask themselves throughout their lives. It's also one that many people will attempt to answer for those who ask it.

Whether from the scientific, the philosophical, or the theological, there is no want for answers that can be adopted as your own. And, if you're lucky, maybe one of them fits you just right. But, interestingly, what is more often the case is that the only person who can *truly* answer that question for you, is *you*.

That can be either a pleasure or a frustration, depending on how you go about it. For the final portion of this book, we will explore some of the ways that people have used to find their meaning, and pitfalls to avoid having your purpose shoehorned upon you.

One summer's day, I found myself outside, sitting on a step and daydreaming for some time. While calmly and absently looking down, I noticed a singular, small ant walking through the rocks of the gravel driveway at my feet.

My focus shifted from whatever I was musing about to this tiny insect as I witness its efforts. I'm not sure what the goal of this creature was at the moment, but for the fact that it seemed relentless in its travels, moving this way and that. Ever moving and never pausing.

After a minute or so of observation, I found myself considering what it was like for this solitary ant in its daily life. Because, knowing what we do about ants, a fascinating and enigmatic dichotomy exists depending how you view them.

As a colony, they act as a collective. They're what is considered a "superorganism". A group of communal creatures that work as a whole to create something that no individual could do themselves. The same is true of bees and termites.

Where the puzzling dichotomy exists is that no single ant understands the totality of what they are individually doing. As a colony, they reliably and inevitably construct an intricate underground nest, complete with air shafts, food stores and a queen's layer. It's a natural marvel of engineering that no one ant could possible understand at every level of its sophistication. And yet, its construction nevertheless materialized through the community efforts of otherwise unknowing individuals.

And so, as I witnessed this ant in front of me — a single that belonged to a multitude — I asked myself, what is it that drives this creature to so fervently carry out its daily tasks? There is no task master forcing it. It's not taking breaks to relax once out of view of the collective. And it cannot possibly understand the totality of what its part in the community is for.

It was at that point, while attempting to place myself in the mind of an ant, that it struck me. At whatever level they experience their lives, each ant must have an intrinsic desire to do what it's doing. To each individual, it's not a task, it's the thing they most want to do. Not the threat of what happens if they don't, and not some other ant levering an action out of this one. No. What I was witnessing was this lowly creature living its life in each moment doing what it most desires to do above all other things!

That must be what motivates these creatures on the individual level. People may call it instinct, and there is a part for that to play. But, the outcome of fulfilling that instinctual desire must be the fulfillment that would drive each ant towards,what would wind up building, a utopia for the community who are all doing the same.

In the short time it took me to watch this minuscule life interacting with its environment, I had unwittingly stumbled upon one of the greatest insights of my own life. One of the focuses of western society is to exemplify each individual person's uniqueness. It's between a person's myriad proclivities and talents, and the degrees to which each presents themselves, that creates a sort of personality fingerprint. Although the hardware we all use is largely the same, it's in the small but important unique qualities where individuality resides. Through the discovery of these personal desires, we inevitably come across activities that give us a sense of fulfillment. It's in these personal discoveries that the hints of purpose reside.

In 1943, psychologist Abraham Maslow proposed a hierarchical chart of what a human needs to feel fulfilled. Often times this chart is contextualized as a stratified pyramid. This concept, referred to a Maslow's Hierarchy of Needs, conveys both what is necessary for human survival (thus, the most base layers of the pyramid) as well as what is accessible for human flourishing once the base layer needs are met. At the bottom levels of the pyramid are things like nutritional needs, security needs and psychological needs. These layers are universally required as "survival" level needs. You simply will not have the ability to move past these on a day to day basis until they are met. Beyond those base layers, once they have been sufficiently met, you are able to access the levels of needs that speak more to the fulfillment your consciousness craves.

Although many if not all of the lower level needs are often met fully in first world societies, there's a societal level mistake that gets made by most people after that point. Due to the necessity of a functioning sociological infrastructure to be able to provide those lower level needs to the masses, the cogs of that machine must be propelled some way. And the way they are, are by the labors of the very same people they enable to rise above them. In this way, a closed loop begins that can last a person their entire life.

There is a saying in business that if you aren't working for your dreams, you're working for someone else's. And that someone isn't apt to enlighten you to do what they are doing if it benefits them for you not to.

You see, in the same way that a colony of ants works differently than an individual — yet is comprised of individuals — there are different dynamics at work (with their own goals) as you pull the lens in or out on society. What so often happens is a misappropriation of goals when the individual in our society works towards the desires of the mass. The difference between a society of people and each person within it are as different (yet interconnected) as the individual ant is from the goals of the colony. They are necessary to each other in very much the same super organizational way, but a problem occurs when you believe as an individual that your goals are that of the society.

This is why we've built an economic mechanism to bind the two together. It's a universal "desire" that can be applied to the individual at the mass societal level. And while this economic mechanism, money, serves that valuable purpose — to drive the individual to serve the needs of the communal — what is functionally happening is a hijacking of the mind of the ant. It's a pseudo synthesis empowering a gatekeeping mechanism that, in reality, is more of an accepted ransoming of your individual desires. Put more plainly, individuals mistake the pursuit and acquisition of money (beyond its requisite function of fulfilling the base level needs of Maslow's hierarchy) as their pursuit for fulfillment. They confuse its function for provision as the end goal of their personal desires.

In this way, many people are raised by a system that is benefited by them fulfilling needs that serve their societal function to the exclusion of their higher level, personal needs. This becomes the closed loop that holds most people within its viscous cycle. Like an animal incited to perform actions that serve another for the chance to be fed. People will live their entire lives missing the point of their lives entirely.

Now, that's not to say that a free and open capitalistic society isn't beneficial. Or that money in and of itself is a poisonous construct. In fact, it seems to be vital the larger a communal system gets. But your *purpose* is not to just to acquire money to the Nth degree. In a society that holds wealth *acquisition* as the metric of fulfillment, common detrimental pitfalls arise in its pursuit. It's an age old phrase, "money can't buy happiness.". The stories, both real and fictional, are plentiful of this particular pitfall. In fact, perhaps the best encapsulation of the myopic belief of people who think it *does* was a quote from the first American billionaire J.D. Rockefeller who famously said, "How much money does it take to make a man happy? Just one more dollar.". Those words came from a man so far beyond the need to acquire wealth that it speaks directly to the hijacking of purpose that so often happens when people mistake gaining money for their purpose.

But even if someone isn't living for excessive acquisition, there can be a false sense of accomplishment that stagnates them in place and prevents them from pursuing what actually brings them fulfillment. Because if society places primacy on money and you have a job doing something you aren't passionate about that provides it, that's considered a net win by most. There is a time and place for doing work that you don't enjoy or even hate, and we'll cover that in the next couple chapters. For the sake of this chapter's focus, it's important to recognize what commonly prevents people from finding their own, individual purpose.

It's my belief that through the process of discovering your own "mind of the ant" (the things that you would rather do more than anything; that brings you undeniable fulfillment) that society is advanced and edified communally as people passionately follow what really drives them. In the same way that each ant within the superorganism is following what most fulfills it, it's my belief that the superorganism that is humanity on a global scale benefits the more people are empowered and enlightened to find and follow their purpose.

20

BREAKING THE CYCLE

"Man cannot remake himself without suffering, for he is both the marble and the sculptor."

— ALEXIS CARREL

I t's an ambitious thing to speak to the meaning of life or your personal purpose within it. If the previous chapter started you thinking along those lines, that's the beginning of finding your own answer. Because what I cannot do, is tell anyone what their purpose is. What I can do, is to offer suggestions to you for which direction to start your search.

In that manner, many people reading may have already answered for themselves what it is that they most want to do at any given moment. The answer to that question is both as simple in theory as it is difficult in practice.

In this chapter we will lay bare the ever present option to not only discover your purpose, but choose to pursue it — whatever the cost.

If, through some act of incomprehensible charity, someone were to gift you with one hundred billion dollars, what would you do with the rest of your life? Surely, there would be a wild rush of ideas through anyone's head about what they could buy, or do, or access with that fantastic amount of wealth. And I'm sure we would all satiate whatever goals we've been working towards for lack of money. But, much like Alan Watts' dream thought experiment in chapter fifteen, there would come a point after that carnal utopia where we'd have to come to grips with the hijacking of our purpose that caused us to see money as the central goal in life.

So the question would stand, "What would you do with the rest of your life?".

The reason for this question is to allow you to pull down the societal facade of goals that were primarily foisted upon you (by threat for want or as reward for good labor) to encourage your efforts in furthering the communal system. But what happens when you disarm these sticks and carrots of their effect, is a return to the question of what matters most to you. And it's important that you be able to answer this question without peripheral concerns like how they may provide your base level needs.

For about fifteen years I worked in the trades as a journeyman welder. I was employed by a dozen different companies for my skills and worked with many different co-workers from a variety of differing backgrounds. Language, culture, upbringing — it was a melting pot of all sorts of people and lifestyles. But one thing I noticed whenever I would ask one of them what their ambitions were, was they would all have an answer that wasn't what they were doing. Though, half the time they may include the skills they were using in the present job, no one could honestly say they were doing the thing they most wanted to do. Besides the fact that they may not have known how to actuate that dream as a reality (which we'll speak to more in the next chapter), it's intriguing to note that they had all run that dream scenario in their minds before. What's more, some of them would go home from a twelve hour work day to spend an hour or two in their garage to work on something they truly loved. One welder in particular (I remember vividly to this day) told me how much he loved to create hand made wooden furniture at home. He already knew what (at least part of) his purpose was. He knew what it was, and he knew what it wasn't. Yet he continued to persist doing what he knew he wasn't passionate about in the belief that he couldn't ever do the same for the thing he was.

There is a pernicious trap that is built through the structures of society, meant to permanently ensnare the individual towards its ends. Money as a goal is only part of it. It serves as the fuel to keep our labors steady, but another promise arises from our efforts to gain it. The promise of luxury and ease if we work hard enough and long enough doing something that's not our personal purpose. While in the work force, this promise gets incrementally kept as you climb a little higher up the ladder of seniority, yearly pay raises, and administrative progression. With every bit of progress that offers a little more income, luxuries that were previously unavailable open up: a bigger house, a nicer car, fancier clothes. And as that dance between achievement and reward progresses, you become the architect of your own trap. Like a prey animal following a trail of crumbs into a cage, we stray so far away from what edifies us to fulfill what edifies society. And at a certain point we don't believe we can do anything else. And in a real way, it becomes a self perpetuating struggle in which our luxuries demand our efforts just for their sake. This is a form of conundrum called the "Golden Handcuffs". We become shackled by our efforts without any lateral options of escape. To do anything else — like spend more than a morsel of time on a passion for woodworking — would cause the collapse of the lifestyle we've built upon our efforts in the rat race.

Rat Park

In the late 1970s, a Canadian psychologist named Bruce K. Alexander, proposed an experiment involving lab rats and morphine. In an attempt to test the "Chemical hook" theory of drug addiction, he added morphine (an analog for heroin) to their water bottles to see how it would affect their behavior. And not just their acute behavior while high, but their chronic behavior in regards to dependency on the chemical.

On one side of the experiment, Alexander observed what would have been expected. All of the rats seemed to develop an addiction to the morphine water. They began continually self administering the drug to the degree that they would sometimes stop eating altogether when they had unlimited access to it.

Their whole lives were contingent upon that drug. Which seemed to solidify the presumption of a chemical hook that overruled their capacity towards moderation or restraint. But this was only one side of the experiment. And on this side, indeed the rats whole lives appeared to revolve around the drug, because what more was there to be offered in contrast? They were lab rats. They existed in a small, individual cage. There's not much in the way of joy or satisfaction beyond some food pellets now and again. But, a counter construct was built that would either prove or disprove the idea of the chemical hook in these rats by comparison. It was dubbed: Rat park.

Rat park was meant to offer the rats everything that a rat desired. An area over two-hundred times the space of their cages. Fully furnished with areas to play, hide, mate, explore — everything that would satisfy what it was to be a rat. The rats on this side of the experiment could enjoy their lives without want for anything. Interestingly, in the area where they would eat and drink, the researchers placed two water bottles. One with the morphine in it and one without. If the chemical hook model of addiction were true, once they tried the morphine water, even while in paradise, they too would succumb to the undeniable addictive qualities of it.

After observing the rats in rat park long enough though, it didn't seem like any of them were addicted, or even unhealthy. As it turned out, when allowed to do the things they most wanted to do, rats would drink the normal water more often than the morphine laced one. And those that would drink the morphine water would only do so every now and again. There was no addiction. It was just considered another experience among many in their park to explore.

What's more, after fifty-seven days on the first side of the experiment, Alexander took all of those rats from their small isolated cages and placed them instead into rat park. Every one of those rats would be presumed fully addicted to the morphine water. But, once in rat park, they voluntarily chose withdrawal from the drug while drinking normal water from the bottle beside it. When given the option of a fulfilled life, they were willing to suffer the literal pain of separation from an unnaturally constrained one.

The Natural Choice

When viewing the rat park experiment objectively as an analogy to finding our purpose, everyone can understand why they would chose fulfillment over a synthetic coping mechanism. But then why is it that, subjectively, we find it impossible to make the same decision for ourselves? We find ourselves working in unnatural and unfulfilling jobs for the promise of a few more hits of a coping mechanism that we need to continue doing what we loath. I haven't checked back on my co-worker from years ago, but I feel safe in the assumption that he's not living out his passion for wood-working. He, like most of us, is likely resigned to continue in a labor he despises instead of breaking the cycle that's brought him to where he is. But for the fear of the unknown, he's willing to live a lie to pay the bills.

How many death beds have been filled by people wishing they could go back to every moment they had the chance to break that cycle? Within the safety of their careers they found a solid floor beneath them with a glass ceiling above them. All the while unaware that it was a gilded cage. And even while they clearly recognize the glass ceiling above that prevents them from their dreams, they know that to break it will also remove the solid floor beneath.

As someone who's personally made the choice more than once to test the unknown at the expense of financial security and synthetic safety, I've experienced what is meant by the saying "Necessity is the mother of all innovation.". Yes, the floor will fall out beneath you in an effort to break your own glass ceiling. And yes, there will be struggle and suffering and insecurity when it does. But the thing I've found time and time again, is that you don't have to find the motivation when you're doing the thing you most love. You will work harder than you did at any job that's trapped you in the past. Once you've not only found your purpose, but committed to it, that is where meaning and fulfillment reside. And I'm not alone in this revelation. Everyone I've talked to who's done the same thing are like the addicted rats who found their way to rat park. We would *all* rather the suffering of withdrawal from our coping cages than to ever return to them now that the walls have opened up around us.

And like I'd stated at the beginning of this chapter, I cannot tell you what your purpose is. But I'm willing to bet that if you don't already have a sense of it, it's not that far away from you discovering it on your own.

In the final chapter of section one, we will explore the many different seasons of life and how they all align to guide you towards the purposes available for you to fulfill and which, in turn, fulfill you.

21

SEASONS

"Every stage of life has its troubles, and no man is content with his own age."

— DECIMIUS MAGNUS AUSONIUS

I f finding your purpose and recognizing the repetitive cycle most people are trapped in were enough, I could stop writing at this point. I believe the previous two chapters should fully illuminate those two important aspects of purpose. But life is not just one thing, there are many different stages to it. So, to say you found a purpose in your life may wind up being a short term thing if you don't recognize the stages of life and their importance in enabling yourself to live fulfilled throughout it.

It could be that you're early in these stages and have the opportunity to learn before the need to implement your visions. Or, it may be that you're late to this knowledge (as I was) and need to re-address where you are in your life in contrast to it.

In this chapter we will first explore the many common ways to view life at a macroscopic level, and then use that knowledge to our advantage. Because, as will become clear, there is a progression within human life — much like the seasons — that must be understood and cannot be hurried.

Generally speaking, a human being will live and die between the span of a day and a century. Though the averages vary by society and technology, even if the average age of death were seventy-five, no one has any guarantees they will get there. But, for those that do, a uniquely valuable vantage is garnered. It seems to be a human level flaw that we tend to see most clearly retrospectively. But, because that seems to be universally true, the wisdom of our elders has long served the purpose of a guiding path. If not directly, personally applicable, then broadly true for those younger than they who are willing to learn. And what people have seen from looking back on a life lived are several important stages of life, starting right from the moment of birth.

The first eighteen years, in western societies, are what tend to set the foundations for the remainder of one's life going forward. They're seen as the "formative" years. And though many individual portions and important benchmarks occur in this stage of life, I'll presume that most readers will have already passed it. That's not to say that there isn't an enormous amount of value to be found in retroactively discovering our own personal ideas and paradigms that were built and set in this period. But I'll leave those specific focuses for the psychotherapists of the world whom delve deeply into it. For the sake of this book, we will consider the early years, those formative eighteen, as a single season in life. The purpose of which is primarily to prepare a child to enter society as a self sufficient adult.

One of the perennial indictments on this season (and it's a fair one) is that, through the schoolroom routines, we are less preparing children to be self sufficient and more indoctrinating them to become workplace automatons. It is, in fact, the very purpose for the format of the publicly funded American grade school programs that so many other western countries mirror. The methodology of memorization and repetition over open discourse and critical thinking. The eight hour school day, complete with work breaks (recess) and lunch times, punctuated by a bell to alert children to the start and stop of each period. This was not a coincidence, it was entirely purposeful. And we have one man, above all others, to thank for it.

In the early 1900s, business tycoon J.D. Rockefeller (the same man quoted in the previous chapter regarding happiness as being one more dollar) founded the General Education Board (GEB) in America. It provided major funding to schools across the country with a particular focus on state run school programs. It was no secret why he was doing this. Rockefeller himself is quoted saying, "I don't want a nation of thinkers, I want a nation of workers.". He would wind up spending an ultimate total cost of $129 million dollars (in the era of the early 20th century) towards this specific aim. A close confidant and business advisor of Rockefeller had the following to say about the GEB's vision of the USA they wanted to invest into building:

"In our dream we have limitless resources, and the people yield themselves with perfect docility to our molding hand. The present educational conventions fade from our minds; and, unhampered by tradition, we work our own good will upon a grateful and responsive rural folk. We shall not try to make these people or any of their children into philosophers or men of learning or of science. We are not to raise up among them authors, orators, poets, or men of letters. We shall not search for embryo great artists, painters, musicians. Nor will we cherish even the humbler ambition to raise up

from among them lawyers, doctors, preachers, statesmen, of whom we now have ample supply."

It's in this understanding of the spirit that was bred into public education that one begins to understand how this formative season of life sets a precedent and trajectory towards that of a good and obedient working class. And it's through this methodology that those who've been raised within it are sent out into their first adult portion of life.

As young adults, most of us cannot see the full picture of the years ahead of us. And why should we be able to? If we were wise we would learn broadly from those who've gone before. But, as the oft cited saying goes, "Youth is wasted on the young.". But there exists, at certain points, a unity between the societal superstructures that exist and the universal seasons of life. At other points, they diverge. And it's important to know where the harmonies reside and at what point to break from the molding of our formative years to work towards our own individual purpose.

So let's begin with the typical human life cycle from the view of the western societal norm. You are born, you are raised, you are then fledged into the workforce where you exist until the retirement age of sixty-five. At that point, hopefully you have enough savings to sustain yourself for another decade or two. Beyond that, you may end up in an elder care facility of some sort until you pass. But, by-and-large, there is no real societal use or value for those past retirement. It's a bleak view of it all, but undeniably and chillingly accurate at the same time.

This is the where much of the macro disassociation between levels of society is conflated. What was described above should not be surprising or confusing to anyone living in such a culture. It's considered normal and acceptable. But, viewing it as a whole, whose goals are being served by this cycle? It's not the individual's. These are societal level goals. But through the ingraining and normalization of this trajectory, most people adopt that prescribed path as their own *individual* one. It is one that holds no value upon an individual's purpose beyond its value to the whole. So long as your actions edify the system, they are considered acceptable and rewarded monetarily in the kind of viscous cycle described in the previous chapter. And though the image being painted above is not one that's flattering to the typical career paths we've all existed within, I want to re-examine this premise for what is valuable to the individual and then present an actionable option to utilize that value to instead serve you within the society, instead of only serving the society itself.

Four Seasons of Work

Starting from the end of the first season, the formative years, there is a massive chunk of time roughly between nineteen and sixty-five that most people consider a single season of life. You work until you retire, and that's all it is. I not only see this as faulty but inaccurate to a degree that will waste most of the best years anyone has to live. Particularly when you understand that you may not even live to the end of it. There is an ancient Latin saying that's often found in middle ages architecture and gravestones, "Momento Mori.". This roughly translates to "Remember you will die.". It's something that is all too often forgotten and ignored in modern cultures. Remembering you are going to die should serve as motivation not to waste the time we have while we have it. And if the majority of our most vital years are found in this one massive chunk of the "working years", it deserves much more attention that just a singular task to complete.

And so, for the sake of this book and the purpose of this task, I will instead break this chunk of time into four seasons. Each of which roughly a decade long, lasting from twenty to sixty. Ten years is a long enough time to make good on dedicated focuses of effort-for-value that serve you as an individual. What's more, they will be actionable within the broad superstructure of society for the sake of its goals, while still keeping the prime focus upon your own. By doing this, we can locate, pursue and fulfill our individual purposes in a way that edifies ourselves to the core while also serving the societal level needs in a bottom up fashion instead of a top down one. It's my belief that, in this way, we will build the proverbial ant nest of interconnected and harmonious action by way of each ant doing the thing that most motivates them every day.

Season One: From Twenty to Thirty.

These years are a person's first taste of what it is to be an adult. A lot of pressure is put on young adults to quickly find their place in society. They will rush out to do so in certain ways that can burden them for the next decade or two in debt. This, again, is seen not only as normal but laudable by societal standards. And though this season does prepare a person for the ones to come, I don't believe it's in the way that western society says it does. This season, perhaps above all others, is served the greatest by the Rockefeller model of indoctrination. Amidst the many shortcomings of such a system, there is something to be said for the value of embedding an ability to work hard doing things you don't enjoy. It seems counter intuitive to everything I've written so far, but there are at least three important purposes that this function serves and they're primarily useful in this first season.

Firstly, learning the ability to "grind" through tasks and objectives that don't enthrall you will build something that is worth its weight in gold for future endeavours: work ethic. The skill of persistent work towards an end goal, even if it's one that doesn't suit your personal purpose, builds a muscle that cannot be faked and will double its value when you need it further on. In the same way that lifting a weight day in and day out builds a muscle through attrition and endurance, so too is the skill of work ethic built.

Secondly, this season is the best time to build this skill because it's the one among the four that you have the most vitality to do so. The energy of youth is considered a super power the further away from it you age. It's in this time that it's best utilized for the hardest efforts necessary to thrive in the latter seasons when it becomes harder to build. Starting your vocational stage of life off with a good work ethic is an advantage that will pay dividends as time goes on. And if you hadn't already built it in the formative years before this season, now is your chance.

And thirdly, perhaps the most important advantage these skills provide you in this season is the ability to find your purpose through your efforts. And this is the point I believe that the typical Rockefeller style prescription should be broken away from. It's in the rush to find your place in the system, whether for the sake of societal status or monetary benefit, that young adults too quickly root themselves in a path they resign to stay in for the rest of their working lives.

How often have you heard of someone who took out a massive student loan to go into some program they thought would benefit them for the aforementioned advantages, only to give up on it part way through the process or even years after achieving the necessary credentials? I propose instead, that the first season should be used to build a strong work ethic (while in possession of the vitality of youth) and then utilize it to find a path that truly aligns with your individual calling. And it should be considered a respectable part of the process to try out many different vocational options in this time. By doing so, it serves all three advantages listed above.

It builds work ethic by using your youthful vitality while giving your best in a job you realize isn't for you en route to finding a path that edifies you in your efforts. At any point along this path you can get tricked and trapped into the self perpetuating cycle of chapter twenty if the focus shifts from what feeds your passion to merely what feeds your bank account or social status. That's why it becomes incredibly important to be honest with yourself in this first season. If you're indifferent and allow the system to convince you that doing something you hate for the next forty years is not only appropriate but beneficial to you in the end, don't be surprised if at the end of your working life you look back upon it with naught but regret for choosing society's goals over your own.

Season Two: Thirty to Forty.

If the first season was a season of discovery and grinding, the season that follows is one of implementation and actuation of what you've now gained. Season two is a season of building. It's at this point where you begin to learn the skills (often many different skill sets that will stack) to allow you the ability to implement your purpose into reality.

This building season is the point at which you will most likely break free of the Rockefeller styled trajectory. And doing so will be scary and quite possibly painful as certain risks will necessarily come along with diverging off of the beaten path. The good news is this, there has never been an easier time to learn new skills and to use them yourself to build something you probably wouldn't be able to without them. So if the first trepidation you have is an inability to do what needs to be done and that is primarily due to a lack of understanding, this is a quickly resolved issue now in two different and highly accessible ways.

Firstly, there are any number of necessary skills that you will personally have to endeavor to learn and eventually master over time. In the information age we exist in today, if you have an internet connection you can have immediate access to highly pertinent education, specific to your needs and often times for free. Between YouTube, social media channels and low entry mastership courses, you can quickly and effectively learn new skills that can be used to build your vision. In the same way that we all build a version of reality between the things that we learn over time, a proprietary network of skills and goals mixed with your own ideas can be seamlessly meshed into a new creation with the aim of fulfilling your individual purpose. One interesting consideration to note is the idea that if you were to simply read the top ten books that exist on any given subject, by the end of that you'll have gained the specific knowledge of it to a degree that would place you in the top one percent of people in the world. This is where the work ethic you've earned from the previous season will play a large role in providing the necessary momentum to start from a zero point in several necessary skills and endure the grind towards infinite improvement over time.

Secondly, if your dreams and the purpose you pursue require a skill that is either *so* far outside of your interests or requires much more time and effort than it's worth between everything else you need to build, there's a way to gain it anyways. This is a simple, obvious yet incredibly valuable trick to leveling up your aspirations faster than you could on your own. And it's simply by not doing it on your own. A mentor of mine, in my late twenties, gave me this piece of advice that's served me time and time again in many different purpose driven projects. He said, "Never try to be a professional at something a professional can do for you.". Because, if you need a part of your creation to be at a professional level, for the time it takes you to master a new skill, you could simply pay a professional to take your project to a professional level *now*. If you posses a low level of graphic design ability, for the price of hiring a pro, your project will present itself as a higher level work with very little requirement from you in the way of time for skill acquisition. It's between a personal balance of those two tips that you will be able (within a relatively short period of time) to create a functional and actuated passion project that moves you in the direction of your purpose. And if you're reading this thinking that it's only with businesses and entrepreneurial goals in mind, you may be looking past the point. No matter what it is that you most want to do, the result of doing that will inevitably produce something of value. Whether it's artistic, mechanical, theoretical or social, what comes from passionate input is valuable output. Often times that value is most readily presented in monetary gain, which is why what I'm explaining probably sounds like it's exclusive to business. But, as will be explained in the next season, even if your endeavors don't lead to monetary wealth, there are innumerable less obvious gains made in the process. Not the least of which is a visceral fulfillment that can only be found doing what you love.

Finally, one last and extremely important point to cover is that this doesn't have to be a zero-sum gamble to start the building process. That is to say, if you (like myself) began this process later into your life and have an entire structure built beneath you from a career you don't love but require to maintain what's been built so far - *do not* drop everything you're doing to start the building process. Think of it in terms of a vertical building. You've built something that's raised you up one-hundred feet above the ground. You cannot simply jump off the roof to start building from the ground up. What you need to do is to build your purpose adjacent to what you've built so far. And then, at a certain point (which will be different for every person), you can span the distance between these two structure with an "off-ramp" that will allow you to safely move out of the life you hate and into the one you love without a total collapse in the process.

For example, if my co-worker, from the previous chapter, were to have been crafting wooden furniture in his garage after each day of working the job he hates with the express goal of turning that passion into his off-ramp - he would be living out his purpose by now. You must be the one to make it important enough to be able to replace your income and life-style before that avenue will ever become possible. And it may be that the passion you're building adjacent to your prison only gets up to half or three-quarters as high as your career. At any point, you can make the decision to enact that off-ramp and switch trajectories. This is the point where things will be scary, but by doing so you will now open up the possible bandwidth for your purpose that was being subsumed by your unwanted career. And a fascinating thing happens when you are now fully in charge of your own success; the fuel of doing what you most want to do will turn into a force multiplier that propels you *much* further than it did when you only had ten percent of your effort available to it.

So, in summation, the second season of these four will be a season for learning, building and self mastery towards what gives you the most joy in life. And through this process, you will be able to create an individualized, self autonomous system that serves you instead of one that uses you.

Season Three: Forty to Fifty.

After you've found and actualized your purpose will come a season of broadening and scaling what you've built so far. This may seem like one single progressive stage from the second to the third, but there are important abilities this season will afford that aren't available in the second, initial building season.

If we were to borrow the analogy from chapter seventeen of higher and lower vibrations, and how certain things only become available within each stratified level; there's a similar truth that exists with a perpetual growth and flourishing of one's purpose. There is a rarefied air that exists atop the higher built passions that few people exist within. This is only accessible to people who've steadfastly and consistently applied themselves to that which most motivates them. So, after an entire season of building, you will find yourself among a small community of like-minded and highly actuated individuals. What becomes possible at this point, simply was not accessible at the lower levels of building your dreams.

In 2002, theoretical biologist Stuart Kauffman presented a biological thesis he called "the adjacent possible". For his purposes, this thesis spoke to a biological entity's ability to move incrementally towards what is immediately beside (or adjacent) to them in an evolutionary sense. This idea was later co- opted and broadened outside the realm of the biological into the sociological and philosophical by author Steven Johnson in his book *Where Good Ideas Come From*. This concept, in the sense of the abstract, speaks to the availability or accessibility of certain things only as we move adjacent to them. For example, if you stand in front of a ladder that leads from the ground onto the roof of a building, you cannot simply move from the bottom all the way to the top. But you can move to the first rung of the ladder as it is the adjacent possibility available to you at the ground level.

Likewise, perhaps half way up the ladder you could access the window of the building that is now the adjacent possible next move that also wasn't an option from the ground or even three rungs previous.

What happens over time as you build your passion projects with consistency and fervor (fueled by your inner purpose) will be an undeniable entry into the strata of people who've done the same. And it's at that point, and not before it, that you are now adjacent to them and their success. This is what causes the ability to broaden and scale your own achievements, because (to invoke an over used business cliché) your *network* equals your net worth. Deals, partnerships, exchanges and networks will open up between passionate, like-minded and driven people that can magnify both party's dreams in a synergistic way that allows for expansions beyond your previous capabilities in the previous seasons.

This is why the third season can be confused for a continuation of the second. Because both are a building process. Like a parabolic arc that starts low, begins to grow and then at a certain point skyrockets exponentially upwards; if season two builds upwards to access previously inaccessible adjacent possibilities, then season three expands your reach laterally to magnify your efforts into something truly magnificent.

And to call back to season two's contention that this isn't only constrained to business styled purposes, once you've built (or mastered) your area of interest (or purpose), the inherent worth of the rarefied mastery will inevitably enable you to do broadly what you couldn't do while building it. For example, if you are a stay-at-home parent that makes no money for their efforts, the building and maturing of those skills necessary to it will bring you to a much more robust (or scaled out) version of that purpose. And the value of that mastery will benefit your society starting directly with your own family and moving outwards from there.

Season Four: Fifty to Sixty.

If the Rockefeller model had one other thing right, it was to present an exit out of the work force before the human body can no longer sustain the efforts its system requires. Similarly, the fourth season of your purpose built working years should be a preparation for you to do the same.

Some people have a very hard time with no longer working, and it's not to say that it even has to be done. But there's another season of life after this one that awaits those who do and is truly only available afterwards. Your opportunity to enjoy it will depend on the preparations you make for the passion built creation you've spent half a lifetime laboring over.

This season requires of you the ability to either automate, delegate or otherwise initiate another off-ramp that allows you to step down from a senior role into a passive one. Sometimes it will be a simple and direct preparation of a successor or group of people capable of taking over. Other times it could be a technological automation that opens the avenue for passivity on your part while maintaining a working apparatus in your stead. Like the process of following your purpose to begin with, there is no generic way of stepping away from a life's work. It's something that will be highly personal and prepared for in a way that honors your vision and the efforts levied to create it. Season four is the time to spend towards those ends if you intend for it to outlast your own time in this life and continue to benefit the ant hill it's being added to. And as was implied earlier, by doing so, you prepare an entrance into the final season of life. One that's more important to those who are to come after you than it is for yourself alone.

The Final Season: The Wise Elder.

After a life well lived, there is a place that exists that only those people can hold in any society. Historically and across many different cultures, it's a place of great honor and looked upon by those before it as a final achievement to attain. This is the position of the wise elder.

In what amounts to our final chance to give purpose and meaning to all of our time and struggles and lessons learned, the position of the elder offers the generations rising up after it access to hard earned wisdom.

And though it's true (as was mentioned at the outset of this chapter), that not all youth will accept the gift of an elder's wisdom, for those that do, untapped possibility becomes freely accessible. And what a gift to give back to those working to follow behind you.

Socrates, like many other wise young men, saw this worth when he implored men to "Employ your time in improving yourself by other men's writings, so that you shall gain easily what others have labored hard for.".

Well Worth The Effort

With the precious short time we have to live out our lives, a curious and honest effort to learn and explore what is available to each of us through the dedicated pursuit of our individual purposes can build a fantastic and interconnected ant hill that benefits us all. At the individual, communal, and global levels.

And though you may still be early in your efforts, it's the *process* and not the end result that really is the purpose that we all yearn for in the end. Do not feel like you can't attempt to reach what lies just outside your grasp for fear of the unknown. In the end, each of us are responsible for what we do with our time. Recognizing what season we're in can at once offer a route towards personal fulfillment.

In section two on purpose, we will dig even deeper into the individual. Instead of focusing on *what* drives us this time, we will discover *who* we even are at the core of it all.

SECTION 2: AUTHENTICITY

22

KNOW THYSELF

"The privilege of a lifetime is to become who you truly are."

— CARL JUNG

There is a lot of work to be done with all of the insights into our purpose that the previous three chapters uncovered. And each piece of each part of them is a very personal process that won't look just like anyone else's version of it. And that's an important aspect of doing it well. It needn't take ten years or forty years for any given season.

Though, it may take even longer. Every bit of the process is a cascade of individualized variables.

But there's another layer to this discovery process that's going to become more essential the longer it takes to resolve. This is a fundamental core anchor that will allow for the processes that need to occur to be approached properly, and with honesty. Like many deep concepts, it sounds as trivial as it is profound in actuality.

It is the question of "Who am I?".

Every single person will need to constantly discover, cherish and defend the answer to that question. Because if you don't know who you are, there are many others who will try to do it for you.

At the very beginning of this book, we started with perhaps the shortest yet most poignant quote of all. Socrates is famously quoted saying, "Know Thyself.". It doesn't sound like a hard thing to do. You are yourself. Who knows you better than you? And yet, though this should ring true, in reality most people spend the vast majority of their lives without ever even considering this once.

Who are you?

In the first formative season of life, before you become an adult, most people decide who they are. And I mean decide;

not discover. There is a huge difference between the two. Through the years of interacting with family, friends, school mates and love interests, an identity is formed that largely mirrors various qualities or pronouncements these people (who are not you) prefer or state as fact about you. And, as an unsure and insecure child or adolescent, we are largely apt to absorb these subjective views as objective truths.

It becomes a patchwork of what people tell us we are, mixed with what we wish ourselves to be that winds up making the identities we tend to maintain as the answer to Socrates' directive. But, more often than not, we wind up being miles away from the truth of the matter. And this is why the work must be done to rectify what amounts to an erroneous datum point. A starting block that isn't even on the race course we intend to run.

There's an age old debate in psychiatry and psychology, one that was mentioned in chapter six when we covered the free will conundrum. It's called the Nature vs. Nurture debate. The crux of the question it's meant to answer stems from a proposed, undefined ratio of importance between the two as they pertain to the building of a person's personality — their wants, needs, desires, proclivities, distastes etc. It's clear that both nature (our genetic predispositions) and nurture (our influential lived experiences) both play a role in the synergy that makes us who we are. The question, of course, is which one is predominant over the other?

As it stands, this debate is more or less at an impasse. The approximate percentages will shift ever so slightly depending who you read, but the most commonly held approximation right now will state that nature accounts for 49% of your personality, while nurture counts for 51%. And though there are many different conclusions that get drawn from these (albeit nebulous) percentages, they serve us for this conversation to make a few particular points.

I'll speak to the nurture side of this first, because there are some built-in assumptions that can lead to immediate false conclusions. Presumably, they come from the use of the word itself; nurture. When using that word, it invokes an image of parental guidance and provision that we as children either had or had not during our formative season. But, in fact, almost none of the aforementioned 51% relates to a parent's part in the rearing of a child at all. The studies most commonly used to come up with this arbitrary number cite *much* more of an influential role of peer groups and random circumstantial experiences. So, in a way, it lets the parents largely off the hook, but at the same time leaves them curiously less important in the overall scheme of personality creation. For the part that they *do* play in the nurture conversation, it primarily revolves around an instantiation of behavioral traits. More or less, the indoctrination of what is or isn't to be understood as socially acceptable behaviors.

For the remainder of this majority percentage, life experiences and the influence of peers account for the prime attributing factors. And I don't argue this pronouncement. In fact, it serves to further illuminate the necessity of the uncovering of who we are that needs to be done.

When we look at the 49% that's attributed to nature, this is where I believe the truth of who we are resides to a large degree. And it's never more noticeable than when we are young. Some of the earliest stages of childhood give us the clearest view of who a human is before they become entangled with who they will wind up being. If you've had the distinct honor of parenting a child, you'll be able to attest to the fact that each baby comes into this world with a unique and pre-loaded personality built into them. Having four of my own, it's remarkably vivid how different they each are from each other, and always were before any outside influences could be added to the equation. And though it's absolutely true that the entirety of our personalities must be taken into account if we are to know ourselves, the intrinsic part of them is firmly rooted in who we were from the start. That is to say, though nurture may account for the democratic majority, it by definition is the malleable side of the whole. While nature remains the unyielding, authentic human being that we always were from the very beginning.

It's because of the difference between these two aspects that our insights into not only knowing who we are, but refining it towards its most pure reflection are found. It's a matter of fact that we cannot undo or remake what we are at the natural, genetic level (at least, at the writing of this book).

Therefore, it should stand that figuring out this part of ourselves should hold primacy. It will represent an anchor that won't change with time and can be called upon if needed. As well as recognized for what it is within any given instance. Conversely, although nurture holds a respectively dominant grasp upon the totality of our personalities, it's within this portion of it that any outside influence can affect not just who we are, but more importantly, who we *think* we are.

In the two chapters to follow, we will spend time to uncover the benefits as well as the detriments of each side of who we are. And, in so doing, be presented with the opportunity to take guiding control of who we are - through the understanding of what is, and what need not be.

23

NURTURE

"If you want to change the world, start with yourself."

— MAHATMA GANDHI

The majority of what makes up our individual personalities, as it turns out, is actually less *us* than it is other people's ideas plus our experiences. That understanding alone should be a revelation to anyone who sees the worth in it. And there's a lot to unpack about this knowledge, both to do with the depth that it goes within us all as well as what can be done about it for our own sake.

As we dig into this incredibly important subject, don't think of what is being written as a user's manual or some sort of directive to be followed. Instead, I would suggest to allow the thoughts in it to spark your own ideas. Because, as with everything that is deeply individualized, only you can discover the value and actions that can be gained from them to be actualized in your own life.

It's an age old trope that we've all been witness to. The middle aged man who still acts like a high school jock. The mother of three who still lives her life like a college sophomore. And as much as it's obvious (to those looking objectively from the outside upon them) that their personalities are hold overs from a generation passed, we broadly neglect many aspects of ourselves that were set years ago and are no longer beneficial to us.

People, being highly social creatures, will mold themselves to their environment to first survive and then second thrive within groups and peers. It's both an innate short term defense mechanism as well as a long term personal detriment that most people don't truly understand while they do it. Like a chameleon in a tree, we take on the appearance of the social environments we're in, so as to not become a target. To stretch the analogy further, we're a green chameleon to move from a green bush to an orange one and unwittingly didn't change its colors, it wouldn't just appear out of sync, but would become detrimental to the creature in the long run.

You see it in early childhood development. Kids are cruel to each other socially. They quickly pick on and ostracize other children who stand out among their peers. And though parents and guardians will try their best to instill a moral compass to counter this, what is happening at this young age is simply an unencumbered mirror of the very same human traits that adults possess and utilize all the time. In fact, this is seen in the animal kingdom all over the place. Birds will attack another of their kind who has a broken wing. Smaller dogs will be picked on and starved by their own siblings. So, it's because of the threat of these actions that people will adapt to morph into what's most suitable or laudable within any given group.

All of these personality adaptations not only affect how we think, behave and react but they compound on top of each other as we move through life. And as they do, they will not just shape who we are externally, but add psychological baggage that can equate to radically different and unexpected results over time. All the while, we become someone that, in reality, can be very far removed from who we are naturally. This can create an internal unease and tension that will lead some people into inevitable psychological torment.

What's more, there are other portions of the "nurture" side of one's personality that add excess, and often damaging, baggage on top of what we choose ourselves. The alterations we take on consciously as a defense mechanism are our choice to make. The remainder of this individualizing portion is filled by the psychological consequences of actions and events that are fully out of our control. These can be as subtle as a bee sting or as overt as an existential struggle. Whether it's the death of a family pet or nearly drowning in a pool — life happens to everyone. And a single event can dramatically affect how we act or view the world and the people within it for the rest of our lives if they're not addressed. The majority of the world's psychiatric practices work towards coming to terms with these unavoidable events that leave psychic scars upon us and transform our personalities to match.

That understanding alone should spark an interest in anyone looking to amend their own personality's dysfunctional portions. Because while we suffer from the baggage that either we've added to ourselves (in an effort to blend in) or have had foisted upon us by no fault of our own — there is an entire, well recognized science to undoing and resetting these parts of our psychology. That should be encouraging. And short of prescribing professional psychiatric care, there are things that we can do for ourselves that can lend to a process of whittling down the vestiges of our nurturing that have walked us so far away from who we authentically are.

I want to take the remainder of this chapter to explore both sides of the nurture equation in an effort to uncover action-able ways that we can work at bringing ourselves closer and closer to who we each individually are. Because, if we can do that, we can not only lessen the tension between who we are and who we project, but we can also resolve our connection between who we are and our individual purpose.

Master of Disguise

The first part of the equation is the part that we're responsible for. And it's the most reasonable part to start with because it was already affected by our conscious effort, therefore, it can be affected by our conscious effort again. And though this may be the simplest way to making a difference in your life, like is often the case — simple doesn't mean easy. To discover what was built in the past that lead to who you are (or act like you are) today, requires a significant amount of honest introspection. And the operative word is honest. We acquired these traits and characteristics within ourselves through dishonesty. We fooled others to think we are a certain way only by fooling ourselves that we actually were. The safety in doing so is self evident, but the comfort we gain in that falsehood will be stripped away when we

force ourselves to be honest to the point of discomfort.

It could be that in the years we've been living a false persona we've not just adopted it as reality, but have subsequently forgotten who we were before we did. And some people, upon coming face to face with the young boy or young girl they first tried to cover up may not even recognize it as themselves when they come back to them. This can cause the shattering of a form of self imposed simulation we've built ourselves into. The side of who we are that we had a say in could stand opposed to the side that was always there. But it's through the dissolution of our preconceived facade that we have an opportunity to come in line with our authentic personhood. The you that was you before others pressured you into someone else.

The encouraging part of this is, wherever it was along the way that who you are diverged towards who you've become can be worked backwards towards your original self. By identifying the parts of you that are not you — those ideas, traits and self-imposed parameters that we absorbed for one reason or another — you can view them for what they are. Did they serve a purpose? Do they still? Do they impede your growth? If so, why do you maintain them?

Because, for this side of the equation at least, *we* are the architect of our persona. Which means, through honest introspection and a mindful diligence towards change, we can nurture *ourselves* towards who we really are. No longer leaving the reins of control up to the pressures of society. If we could nurture ourselves away from who we authentically are, we can also nurture ourselves back towards it.

Observing Adversity

This leaves the remainder of the equation — aggregated traumas. These are all of the imposed events and their damages that we had no say in, yet account for a significant amount of who we've become as a person.

Very often, it's this side of the nurtured aspect of our personalities that create chasms between who we are and who we've become. Sometimes, these chasms cause so deep a rift that the undoing or spanning of them can require a lifetime of continual effort to attain. Most psychiatrists spend the bulk of their time and efforts towards exactly these sorts of repairs. And, as was mentioned earlier, I don't intend to give any sort of psychiatric advice. Even if I had the credentials to (which I certainly don't), I wouldn't do so in a book that could be read by anyone. Such undertakings, like everything to do with our purpose, are an extremely personalized and unique journey. What I can attempt to provide though, are some insights that others have had when it comes to these kinds of scars that separate us from who we really are. Because, no matter who you are, everyone is affected by these kinds of formative traumas. Some are extreme and some less so. But they are a universal variable that mainly differs by degrees. And as such, there exist certain universal truths that can speak into anyone's personal versions of them to one degree or another.

The following insight comes from both the Stoic and the Buddhist traditions. Both of which, in their own ways, come to the realization that we as humans actually have very little control over what happens to us. In the Buddhist philosophy, they put an enormous emphasis on suffering. They believe that to exist as a person implies suffering. The goal of a person, who is bound to suffer in their lives, is to learn to minimize their suffering. And they don't just mean in the physical sense. In fact, many Buddhist traditions would impose physical suffering in the attempt to reduce or conquer mental suffering. They hold what we do mentally that leads towards our own suffering as paramount in importance. Because it is, as they see it, only the self that we can master in any real hope to master internal suffering. And, to the contrary, any attempts a person makes to try and prevent external vectors of suffering in their lives only ensures more internal suffering due to the futility of such efforts. So it is that by the mastering of what we can control — ourselves — we may attain a state of transcendence that goes beyond the physical.

In a similar way, though in a more pragmatic sense, the ancient Stoics of Greece and Rome implored one to observe what is, without being drawn into emotional reactions to it being so. It serves no one to scream at the waves for their crashing against the shore. Their actions hold no bias and simple are what is. This philosophy was presented in a classic fable called the scorpion and the frog. In this tale, a scorpion wished to cross a raging river, but knew if he attempted it he would surely drown. In his pacing of the bank he came across a frog. He implored the frog to help him cross the river to the other side. The frog, not out of malice, first refused him stating, "If you crawl atop my back for the voyage, you would sting me because you're a scorpion.". The scorpion retorted, "Why would I do such a thing? If I stung you while upon your back, we would both drown together.". Seeing the logic in this double jeopardy scenario, the frog finally obliged. Although it would come to pass, that half way across the river, the scorpion succame to his base desires and he stung the frog. The frog, shocked and confused while they both began to sink, said, "Why would you do that? Now we both will drown!". The scorpion could only, in all honesty, reply, "I am a scorpion. It is my nature.".

In the Stoic view of this fable, there is no reason to be angered at the scorpion. He simple did what a scorpion does. And transposed upon our own lives, they believe it folly to hold malice or vindictively begrudge someone who causes you trauma. Their actions were not yours to decide. Perhaps you could learn not to let scorpions on your back in the future, but that wisdom doesn't undo the harm you've suffered already. And psychologically speaking, there's a paradoxical reflecting of harm that we impose upon ourselves by allowing emotional footholds to the actions of people upon us. As horrendous as they may be, by remaining in that place of harm tethered by emotional response, we multiply and exacerbate the harm manyfold in the imme-diate moment and into the future. There's a common adage that says, "Resentment is like taking a poison and waiting for the other person to die.". And though letting go is a much harder ask than it sounds, it really is a large part of what psychotherapy tries to empower trauma victims to do.

Even if you don't personally need a psychiatrist to help you let go of past events, the lesson of the Stoics and the Buddhists can actually even prevent such harm in the future by detaching their hold over who you are. The ability to observe what is, and let it be, is a superpower that many people have worked tirelessly to obtain. But, if it can be obtained, therein lies an avenue to prevent outside affects to obscure who you authentically are.

There is more to the ability to minimize the overall effects of trauma induced personality affectations, but they will be more deeply covered in chapter twenty-seven on suffering. Suffice to say, of the two sides of ones personality (that is largely how we both view the world and allow it to influence us and our decisions), the most change can be applied to the side of nurture. And it should be seen as a blessing that it can be. Because were everything truly outside of our control, insanity should be a reasonable response.

But in the next and final chapter in this section on authenticity, we will look into the other (much more immutable) side of our personality. That of nature. And, although we will be left wanting for an ability to change it, it's within its steadfast stability that we find out so much of who we truly, authentically are.

24

NATURE

"If you cannot trust yourself, you cannot even trust your mistrust of yourself — so that without this underlying trust in the whole system of nature you are simply paralyzed."

— ALAN WATTS

W hat does it mean to be authentic in regards to who you are as a person? On the surface, you might say authenticity is a representation of the unencumbered self. And to a certain degree, that's true. We just spent the last chapter discovering those things that encumber you in the first place. And the unraveling and dissolving of those things that ought not remain is a fundamental first step towards who you authentically are.

But for a person to even *have* something that it is to be authentic, presumes some sort of prima facie form. Some base level, the original *you* that was always there. And if this is the case, than the dissolving of the nurtured effects on your personality should more acutely resolve, uncover and liberate that which they were built upon. This is the nature side of us. And there's a lot more going on there than just the derivative sum of biology. Some people may consider it the soul.

If you are to venture into the studies and their findings within the ongoing debate of nature versus nurture, what you will notice primarily is that the term nature is often synonymized with genetics. Since the discovery and subsequent mapping of the human genome, a profound amount of what people are (and even have the latitude to become) is considered to reside there.

The Genetics

Heritability (the degree to which a trait may be passed from parent to offspring) accounts for many if not all of the physical traits that could be easily studied. If there's a biological structure or unique qualitative physical trait that can be visually quantified, through the processes of selective breeding, it's been shown a matter of arithmetic probability to be the sum of the union of different gene pools. This has been known for hundreds, if not thousands of years before the discovery of DNA.

Obvious traits (like height, hair, eye color and even the shape of earlobes) are easily traced back as heritable derivatives of family trees. This is why your doctor will ask you if there's any history of heart disease in your family during a routine check up. It's also why the pedigree of champion race horses is of utmost importance to horse breeders and gamblers alike. The degree to which physical genetics can be manipulated through genetic heritage is extreme. More extreme, perhaps, than many people even realize. For example, both the minuscule Chihuahua and the massive Great Dane are essentially the same breed of dog. They were each selectively bred from either end of the extreme genetic possibilities within their lineage for height. But although all physiology seems to come down to the coding of our genes, how much of the psychological is naught more than a role of the genetic dice? This is more than just a nebulous question. It's the heart of the nature side of the personality debate. The problem with this question, from a purely empirical standpoint, is how can one *prove* for mental proclivities and predispositions as being the direct result of a symphony of genes? Where and to what degree can one reasonably draw the line between the biological and the environmental?

Thankfully, many ingenuitous biologist have put their minds to exactly this task and have broadly focused on a certain genetic quirk that happens with some children. The technical term for it is monozygotic twining, more commonly know as — identical twins. This happens when a single fertilized egg separates into two in the womb. As far as nature goes, these children serve as a perfect sample for genetic versus environmental dichotomy testing. As both children share exactly the same genetics, any differences between them would automatically be presumed to be environmentally caused.

One particular researcher, a psychologist named Thomas Bouchard, released a hallmark paper in 1990 known as the *Minnesota Study of Twins Reared Apart* (MISTRA). In the MISTRA study, he managed to locate and evaluate over 130 different sets of identical twins who were adopted out to different families at birth. In this way, though the genetic similarities would be identical, the environmental differences would be completely different. Thus, the enigmatic entanglement of nature and nurture at the psychological level could be fully bifurcated and compared.

Many interesting discoveries were made from the MISTRA twins. The most remarkable of all were a set of twin boys referred to as the Jim twins. These identical twin boys were separated at birth to different homes and only reunited at the age of 39. When they were brought together, a shocking amount of similarity was found that defies conventional logic. Although adopted by two different homes at the age of three weeks old (who had no knowledge of the other family beyond the fact that their adopted son had an identical twin somewhere), they oddly wound up living within forty miles of each other. Both parents, without foreknowledge of the others, ended up naming their new babies James. Both James' would wind up being referred to as Jim. Each of them would name their childhood dog Toy. Both had a penchant for woodworking and math but struggled with spelling. By the time they had first met each other, both Jims had married and divorced two women. The first marriage of each was to a woman named Linda, while the second marriage was to women named Betty. The first born son of each twin was named James Alan and James *Allen*. On top of all that impossible serendipity, both brothers took up a heavy smoking habit, both drove a blue Chevrolet car and each went into a law enforcement job.

The story of the Jim twins became an instant pop sensation and made it into the famous catalog of strange stories and oddities — Ripley's Believe it or Not. Although this seems like an unbelievable win for the nature side of the personality debate, they wound up being the only of over 130 twins like them in the MISTRA study that had this level of coincidence. What the more broadly discovered takeaways from this study showed were a fairly undeniable causal link between approximate IQ between the twins. And what's more, the IQ parity seemed unshaken by any span in comparative differences of IQ between the adoptive parents.

Suggesting that IQ was much more robustly affected through the genes than it was parental guidance. They concluded that IQ seems about 70% related to genes, while 30% could be environmental. Things like possible malnourishment, or a lack of optimal schooling can affect the total realized potential of any given child. But other similarly dominant mental traits were proven heavily for nature. Some of which (that were not quite as dominant as IQ but still higher than 50%) were a variety of proclivities like aptitude for music, spacial awareness, and interestingly even religiosity. The latter of which lent less towards any similarity in religion as it did the propensity to take up a religion at all. Interestingly, another odd and seemingly genetic predisposition that was found to have high correlation is a likelihood to divorce. Genetic twins who would have high degrees of otherwise positive traits like how joyful, emotional, impulsive and engaged with life they were, paradoxically, would be much more likely to end their marriages in the future.

Now, before we rubber stamp everything that is our natural personality as completely genetic, I want to dig a little deeper into first the scientific, then the philosophical and finally the theological sides of this focus.

Two things about the science of genetics as they pertain to individuality should be stated and then demystified. Firstly, when genetic evidence was originally being considered as admissible in a court of law in the United States back in the

90s, deterministic mathematics resolved the possibility of a naturally occurring exact genetic match between two different humans as a 1 in 19 billion person chance. Although that stands as over two times the present 8 billion person population of the earth, it's not so far removed as to reasonably consider that you may have an exact genetic duplicate out there that you'll never know about. So far as the societal implications of that are concerned, there are obvious problems that may occasionally arise as both facial recognition and other biometric security implements become more prevalent across the world. False positives in the courtroom cannot mathematically be considered impossible. But to come back to the personality question, judging off of the findings of studies like the MISTRA one, if you did have a genetic duplicate out there, they may be as authentically you as you.

The second thing to consider is the level of codependent interaction within the human genome. That is to say, there doesn't seem to be a single gene that determines anything on its own. Certainly nothing at a systemic level. In the same way that memories are a collection of interactions between a variety of desperate nodes, so too (it appears) is the interaction within our total genome. This was discovered to the chagrin of the researchers who originally mapped the human genome around the turn of the century. They had hoped to very quickly find all of the important buttons and levers to adjust to take full control of human biological expression. What they found out instead was that to change one thing within the whole caused an unexpectedly entangled cascade of effects upon the system as a result. But what this functionally means to each of us as individuals is, even if the majority of our genetics are similar to someone else's (barring a complete clone), the difference between us makes all the difference. As the degree of change within a differing system (even if the differences are small) make for a dramatically varied outcome between the two. So what that means for you, is that your genetic uniqueness is almost certainly otherwise unrealized by anyone else on earth.

So on one hand, there does stand a chance that we all may have what amounts to a monozygotic twin out there, so far as our genome is concerned. But on the other hand, any minor degree of difference between you and every other person on earth accounts for what realistically provides a unique and biologically distinctive naturally occurring authentic you.

If instead we move this into the philosophical realm, then considerations of biology start to diminish in importance compared to other non-scientific ones. Take the first nine chapters of this book for instance. Most every construct and concept regarding consciousness would speak right passed the degree of similarity our radios have in their nuts and bolts if the lion's share of what gives us an experiential existence resides within the signal it receives. Now someone may look at that contention and ask, "But what of all the similarities of personality seen in twin studies?".

Philosophically, those contentions would fall within the same considerations as the Dawkinsian hammer example. Where Dawkins would say consciousness is clearly a biological result of a working brain as could be witnessed by hitting someone in the head with a hammer and noticing their conscious thought processes diminish from it. As from the dualistic analogy of a radio and signal, all the hammer would prove would be that a damaged radio doesn't receive the signal as well. So too, in the case of genetic twins, would their likeness display a similarity in how the hardware projects a signal it receives. There may be (in a Descartesian substance dualistic construct) an interactive factor that varies the ability and presentation of consciousness in tandem with the body side of the mind-body union. Or it may be that some other important variable about the signal side of the equation could account for variance between identical biology and their uniqueness at the personality level. Questions like "Is all consciousness one fluid signal?". And "Does each person entwine with a unique conscious counterpart?" need to be considered. If it were the former, identical natural personality would likely follow. Though, if it were the latter, the individuality of the conscious counterpart could play into a variance in the nature side of identical twin's personalities. None of this (like most everything outside of science) can be proven for or against. Which is why it necessarily needs to be left in the hands of philosophy. But there is another consideration, that should be added to the conversation, that falls outside of the realms of both the scientific and philosophical.

There is a theological aspect to any holistic conversation about nature. For in the theological sense, there is a spiritual conversation that seems to either subsume the side of consciousness or add another layer to its ethereal considerations.

All of the Abrahamic traditions expressly speak to the existence and importance of the soul. It's considered to be a uniquely individual aspect of any given human. Both created from and bequeathed by the one universal God. In this paradigm it goes without saying that no matter the genetic similarity, even including identical twins, each single human being has a unique, one of a kind soul. And it's this variable that is considered *the* paramount vector of what would be a person's authentic self. Before any influencing pressure of the world could affect a change upon it, the soul was purpose made and unique at the beginning of every human's existence.

If this were what Descartes was seeing as a separate but entangled consciousness of unknown origin but substantial importance, then it could be that the natural, immutable version of ourselves is both of and from a single source — while still unique in its creation and affectations. This is actually curiously similar to the Hindu belief of Brahman, the one prevailing consciousness that *is* everything and experiences itself through every individual iteration it projects inside its universal simulation. And then again, the similarities continue into the simulated multiverse construct as even at the quantum level, we produce infinite individual, unique versions of ourselves and our universe with every collapse of the wave function.

It could be that what all of the scientific, philosophical, and theological practices are saying about our uniqueness, are just different ways of quantifying what it is that makes us individually authentic to ourselves.

And no matter what it is in the end that causes or accounts for who we always were, beneath the layered exterior of life events and psychological morphisms, I believe that it's within this true self we will find what we need to harmonize our efforts with. And in so doing, unify the quality of our causes with the primacy of our purpose. A purpose that has always been there to discover and actualize.

In our final section of the final portion of this book, we will explore what is necessary to take action towards and stay the course in our efforts of a purpose driven life. For even if you discover your purpose after resolving who you authentically are, to be able to carry on towards it, in spite of anyone or anything that would deter you, you must first become sovereign.

SECTION 3: SOVEREIGNTY

25

MASTERING THE SELF

"You have power over your mind — not outside events. Realize this, and you will find strength."

— MARCUS AURELIUS

In the process of figuring out who you authentically are, all sorts of ugly and damaged parts of who you presently are will arise. It's not a small task to shed light upon everything that has built who you are today and retroactively reform them.

Considering the two portions of personality we've just covered, addressing both of them in their own way is the only course towards being in control of yourself. Because, as the Buddhists and the Stoics both remind us, we are the only thing that we *can* control. Therefore, it becomes imperative for us to truly master that which is the only thing we control. Doing so will not only present you the latitude to be free in your pursuit of personal purpose, but to become maximally resilient towards all that cannot be controlled. This is what it is to be sovereign.

Every day, there is a war that rages inside our minds. It's not a war that can be won, but it's one that anyone with the goal of mastering their mind *must* fight. This war isn't even about winning so much as it is about not losing. And your adversary is one that will exist as long as you do, because they *are* you.

Both the nature and the nurture sides of your personality lend aid to what is an internal conflict in their own ways. That aid can be towards one side or the other depending on the work that you do to control them. It's for this reason that any effort to gain control over one's inner self is by nature a temporary one. Something that must be perpetually paid mind and intention to if you hope to maintain mastership of yourself.

On the side of the nurtured projections of our personalities, this battlefield is one that's ever changing. The difficulty in any efforts to control it are largely in the continuous evaluating and re-evaluating of what environmental factors are being absorbed by and projected though you. If after reading through the section on authenticity you took the time to consider what parts of you are not you and whether or not they serve you or harm you, that's great. But that work isn't a one time thing. In the same way that lifting a heavy weight once doesn't build any significant strength, doing inner work with honest introspection is a repetitive, perpetual process. But in the same way that repetitive lifting of a heavy weight increases your ability to do so over time, so too does consistency benefit the minds of those who question their own motives and actions. By doing so, not only can you stay on top of controlling how much external pressure or environmental influence can internally reside, but you build a proverbial muscle that makes it easier to do as a habit.

On the side of the natural projections of your personality, this has its own similar but different issue as the nurtured side. Where in the case of environmental effects there's a priority on tracking various ever changing pieces, with the natural side of the equation, things don't change at all — which is its own sort of problem. While most anything about you that was spawned from an external force can be isolated and rectified, anything about your natural side, by nature, cannot be changed. So if there are what amount to character

flaws in what it is to be you — traits like narcissism, patho-
logical lying, or even sociopathy or psychopathy — those
cannot be removed in the same way that an environmental
effect can be. What it comes down to to gain mastery over
our authentic selves, both the good and the bad, is knowledge of who we are and a steadfast effort to minimize the
bad while maximizing the good. Because, as the Stoics would
point out, we cannot change that which is, only how we react
to it. This even includes the parts of *us* that simple are.
Conversely, if the understanding is never achieved of who
you naturally, individually are, you won't even realize what it
is you're reacting to before you've reacted. Often time people
will justify it as an outside affect and miss the internal cause
altogether. For instance, if someone were to cut you off in
traffic, it seems correct for you to express anger. Cursing
and muttering was something they caused you to do, right?
Maybe though, it's the case that you have a naturally low
threshold for personal slights, and you always have. If that's
the case, were the same thing to happen to someone who has
a much higher threshold, they may not even feel the inclina-
tion to shout and rant. So, in which case was the person who
got cut off made to express anger? Objectively, it was
neither. But it would require more personal work from
someone with a lower threshold than it would from
someone without that natural tendency. This is the constant
struggle with mastering our nature. It will always be there.
Any attempts towards mastery are not to try and change
them, but to recognize they're there and measure our reac-

tions to them appropriately.

In both cases (whether the side of who you are that is malleable or the side that's immutable), by using the knowledge of who you are, you must vigilantly preen what can be changed and tame what cannot. This is the war. But we've only spoken to what and how to *master* your inner self. There's an opposite side to this war that you can switch to at any point. In fact, it's the default position to take.

While we are able to take action in understanding and mastering ourselves, any lull in that effort (all the way up to a complete absence of it) will leave you in the throws of the base effects of its antithesis. In the environmental arena, we can simply react to outside pressure as if we've no agency. Play the victim of circumstance. After all, we had no control over what happened to us. Therefore, we can decide that the easiest and most reasonable conclusion is to kowtow and wilt under its pressure. Or in the case of our natural selves, it's simply who we are. We can't be expected to change it, therefore, the simplest and most efficient course of action is to blame our shortcomings as an inevitable effect of our flawed nature. The fact remains, both options are there for you to assume. One or the other. Every time. This is both a caution and an opportunity.

There is an ancient story that was passed down through the oral traditions of the Cherokee tribes of North America. It spoke very plainly to this internal dichotomy through a simple yet poignant tale know as The Two Wolves. The story goes as such:

A young boy came to his Grandfather, filled with anger at another boy who had done him an injustice.
The old Grandfather said to his grandson, "Let me tell you a story. I too, at times, have felt a great hate for those that have taken so much, with no sorrow for what they do. I have struggled with these feelings many times."

"It is as if there are two wolves inside me; one wolf is good and does no harm. He lives in harmony with all around him and does not take offense when no offense was intended. He will only fight when it is right to do so, and in the right way. But the other wolf, is full of anger. The littlest thing will set him into a fit of temper." "He fights everyone, all the time, for no reason. He cannot think because his anger and hate are so great. It is helpless anger, because his anger will change nothing. Sometimes it is hard to live with these two wolves inside me, because both
of the wolves try to dominate my spirit."
The boy looked intently into his Grandfather's eyes and asked, "Which wolf will win, Grandfather?"
The Grandfather smiled and said, "The one I feed."

Why it matters?

There's nothing new to the concept of choosing between an easy yet detrimental path or a difficult yet rewarding one. It's the story of these decisions piled atop each other over time that have made individuals who they are and civilizations what they became. From the transition of the hunter gatherer into the agrarian culture, or the stone tablet all the way up to the electronic tablet; staying with the simpler or most obvious choice is entirely possible, but far less beneficial than doing the work towards a better way through time and effort.

But being able to harvest your own food instead of forage for it is a much more objective benefit than internal psychological efforts to control one's self. So what's to gain from personal self mastery? For the amount of constant effort and often egoic pain involved in assessing and controlling each part of your inner self, what harvest is there to benefit us for the work? This is where the value of sovereignty resides. A value so cherished by wise men of the past that it was considered of paramount importance to achieve.

As will become more apparent in the next chapter (and in a similar sense of how an absence of authenticity will be filled by inauthentic replacements), once you are the master of your inner self, there are no outside forces that can shake you without first gaining your express consent to do so. To fully control and maintain sovereignty of your mind offers a form of freedom that is only available to those disciplined enough to earn it. Aristotle stated exactly this over 2300 years ago when he said, "Through discipline comes freedom.". For the efforts necessary (the perpetual discipline required), a person avails themselves the ability to know who they are while reserving the right to express it on their terms and no one else's. The value of this is enormous. But as you'll see in the next chapter, the absence of it can lead to personal calamity.

OUTER SOVEREIGNTY

"No amount of force can control a free man, a man whose mind is free. [...] you can't conquer a free man; the most you can do is kill him."

— ROBERT A. HEINLEIN

F reedom is a fascinating concept. And it *is* a concept. It's something that must be fought for, defended and written into law for any hopes of maintaining it. But there's a misunderstanding when it comes to that maintenance beyond the generation who earned it. For those who fought to free themselves and those they love, there is no question what cost they must be willing to pay. Everything, up to death, must be at wager. Not just to gain freedom, but to fend off advances to take it back once you have. This is where the misunderstanding happens for those who've been given freedom as an inheritance from those who fought, died and earned it through extreme effort and sacrifice. Like the children of a dynasty, they've never known anything but the riches of other's labors. And what happens often at that point is a replacing of reverence for that inheritance with a presumed entitlement to it.

This is how freedoms are lost. When the worth of them is lost. And what it so difficult to realize for those who've never had to do the work, is that there's a precursor to freedom — sovereignty. For lack of that, freedoms are wrenched from the hands of those who never thought they'd see them gone.

The importance behind gaining understanding and control of your self, in itself, is actually not just about the self that's involved. In the sense of chaos theory, the ripples from one event affect other far reaching parts within the total system they started within. In this case, the individual, through the efforts of self mastery, creates ripples out into society that have enormous consequences.

It's through these sovereign, empowered people that entire civilizations can be built or broken for their lack. It tends to lead to a cyclical rise and fall within cultures and empires over time. Through the successes of those best equipped to stand up against malevolent forces, peace and freedom are achieved. Yet under the sanctuary of those who came before, they who follow after find no worth in building themselves as strongly as their predecessors. There's an old, well-worn cliché about this cycle of rise and fall. It goes like this: Hard times build strong men. Strong men build good times. Good times make weak men. Weak men bring hard times.

This is typically how the cycle starts and eventually implodes. But what is it about those "strong men" that give them the ability to build good times? They are, ostensibly, no different from any other person but for one thing. They understand who and what they are and are willing not only to defend it, but die for it rather than allow it stripped from their hands.

But then the question follows, "What makes 'weak men' bring hard times?". Because, to know both of these things is to know where we presently are in the cycle, and also what must be done at any of the four points within it. What it comes down to in the final stages of societal collapse, in my estimation, is the following. Those who came before and earned the good times are either long gone, or faded out of prominence. Replaced in their stead by a majority of entitled beneficiaries who don't even understand the worth of what they were given. When worth is lost, in anything, that thing will no longer be valued, coveted or protected with the vigor necessary to prevent those who realize its worth from (either by force or by negotiation) relieving you of it.

This is where laws tend to try and bind those valuable societal structures in place beyond when they who built them are no longer around. But over time, even laws will change. Because, those charged with upholding them also change over time and become infiltrated by the same weak men that bring hard times. This is how you can clearly see that freedom is a concept. It's the result of incredible efforts by sovereign individuals who cannot be forced out of who they know they are. You don't get freedom, at any level, without personal sovereignty. And that is something that can only be earned by the individual, and once so, cannot be stolen away.

Mass Formation and Diffusion of Responsibility

Many times over human history, entire populations have fallen prey to those who prey upon the weakness of weak men. That is, those people who immediately falter under pressure. There exists in the human psyche, a quirk. One that starts with an individual, but soon after spreads within massive groups. We already know from our digging into the nurture side of our personalities that humans have a natural defense mechanism that leads them to assume the dynamics of the group they hope to belong to. You can call it peer pressure, but really, peers have very little ability to cause acquiescence unless the mind of those they pressure is willing to allow for it. And so you can see how, at a societal level, when an abundance of mentally weakened individuals come under a united pressure, they not only will wilt beneath it, but pressure those around them to do so as well.

It becomes a chain reaction of allowance that starts climbing up the ladder of the weak in society until it meets the resistance of the strong. The problem being, when the weak out number the strong at a massive level, they become a weapon of mass control by those who wield the united pressure that formed them into a singular mob to begin with.

It's been seen throughout time. Whether in the middle ages, during the inquisition, where the fear of witches among the people cause those people to turn upon each other. Or in Stalinist Russia, where the pressures of being deemed a counter revolutionary saw the gulags filled with every kind of innocent person. Even more recently during a world wide pandemic that wound up turning friends and family against each other, across the globe, out of fear. This is a human trait that becomes calamitous when enough of a population is so susceptible to outside pressures that who they are as an individual gets eclipsed by the mass.

During the pandemic, Belgian professor of psychology at the university of Ghent — Mattias Desmet — came to global prominence regarding a thesis that spoke directly to this mob creation dynamic. He coined it as "Mass Formation" and detailed his view of its mechanisms and causes on various podcasts as well a book that he wrote called *The Psychology of Totalitarianism.* In his view of mass formation, he contends that a society under pressure will form into three groups. 30% will be quick to fold under the pressure, 30% will hold fast beneath it, and 40% will remain agnostic of either of their stances. To be able to form a mass that can be wielded by a totalitarian, the fight is over the moderates in the 40%. Because, if they can be convinced (by carrot or by stick) to join those that folded, at a certain point the original wilted 30% become a majority.

The resulting mass that is formed acts as a group due to the individual propensity people have of following the social prescriptions of their peers. Especially if they are reinforced with fear and repercussion towards those who don't. At that point, any totalitarian who can wield the scepter of fear that drove the mass to form in the first place, has at their disposal a bludgeon to smash those who would not join it.

There is a strangely analogous communal quirk that exists in another part of the natural world. It happens in a select few species of grasshopper. Of those species though, under certain environmental conditions, a radical transformation occurs.

You may have heard stories of biblical plagues of locust, but did you know that locusts are a transformative morph of grasshoppers? Grasshoppers, typically being solitary insects, don't tend to amass into anything resembling a plague. But, in certain areas of the world, when an abnormally lush rainy season produces a bumper crop of these grasshopper's food sources, their populations spike in response. But, what's more, due to the unnaturally high numbers of these insects, they begin to encroach upon each other's stalks of food. When they get close enough to each other to brush the tiny hairs that grow from their hind legs, a biological hormonal reaction is set into effect. In a matter of days, affected grasshoppers will eat, grow and molt into a larger and seemingly mindless versions of their former selves, focused only upon feeding. This transformation cascades throughout the already enormous population and a *mass* transformation occurs forming a plague of locusts that swarm in groups so large as to appear like a dark cloud on the horizon.

This gargantuan horde, at a group level, seems to move as one. They transport en mass from one lush area to the next, decimating them in the process. What's interesting though, is less about the way they move as a whole, and more about why they do so as individuals. Researchers studying these plague dynamics discovered that at the singular level, as one locust hops or flies in front of another, the latter follows it. Not out of allegiance, but in an attempt to *eat* the locust in front of them. So that as the food is demolished by the mass, their prime directive of feeding follows to the next edible thing in front of them. In this way, those behind try to eat those in front who are trying to escape those behind while also chasing those in front. This is where the analogy becomes apparent. Although psychological instead of biological, people will group together out of fear as locusts do out of feast. The pressures of one produce a forwarding affect upon the next in what turns into its own cascade leading towards the formation of a mass. Unlike grasshoppers, though, we have the possibility of resolving against joining a horde. The issue at hand isn't whether or not we can, but whether or not we *have* before those pressures come. And this is where it becomes imperative for each person to do their internal work that fosters a true and steeled mentality *before* that asset is required of them. Like trying to cram for a final exam the night before, you cannot fake what takes dedicated time and effort to produce upon demand. And coming full circle, this is where a society becomes vulnerable to implosion. When the majority of a population is predisposed to follow the group and blend in, whether or not it aligns with who they are, and there aren't enough people mentally strong enough to stand against it — prepare for hard times.

In the end, it comes down to a personal responsibility to yourself. Doing the work. But conversely, those who don't or haven't before the time comes that they need it, they for the price of surrendering their individual sovereignty get to diffuse any personal responsibility onto the group. It's the excuse given in the Nuremberg trials by Nazi commanders after the second world war, "I was just following orders". Personal responsibility, in the moment of action, was transposed upon the mass that was animating and demanding their compliance. Would they have suffered for not following orders? Yes, most definitely. But it comes down to what *you* as a person are willing to do when presented with a directive that runs utterly counter to who you know you are.

This is both the power of and the necessity of fully knowing who you are as a self. And why the more people who do this, individually, wind up creating the bulwark of those strong men that can turn hard times into good times against all odds. This is *always* the way it has to happen, because change cannot be mandated from the top of a society down. It happens in the other direction. By either the acquiescence or the fortitude of the individuals that make up the whole. This is both the reason why totalitarianism can rise as well as why it must eventually fall. An abundance of strong or an abundance of weak, paradoxically creates its own antithesis over time. And depending on the time you find yourself in — whether good or bad, weak or strong — it's only through a personal dedication to gain the sovereign ability to free your mind that you can hope to bring the good or fight what's bad.

Doing so will not only require effort, but inevitably, require suffering. Freedom to be who you are is never free. It must be found, controlled and defended for. Each part of this process will impose its own perpetual degree of suffering. But as we move into the final chapter of this book we will discover that even suffering itself can be mastered in ways that become our strength instead of our weakness.

PURPOSE IN SUFFERING

"Suffering has a noble purpose: the evolution of conscious-ness and the burning up of the ego."

— ECKHART TOLLE

S uffering is the antithesis of flourishing. Isn't that the case? When one suffers, all other cares fade beneath the cloud it casts upon them.

There are so many different ways people suffer, and no one on earth has ever been exempt from it. So much so that it has been broadly considered the enemy of humanity, to be warded off at all costs.

But what *are* the costs in the avoidance of suffering? If it were possible to never suffer again, in anything or any way, would that be beneficial? It's a crude question to ask considering the degree to which many people seem to be needlessly trapped in perpetual anguish. Sometimes of their own making, but other times for no fault of their own.

If suffering is in fact unavoidable, what is there to do about it? Both personally and altruistically. Could we eliminate suffering from life, or could that excise a critical part of what builds a well attuned human being?

In this our final chapter, we will look unabashedly at the trials of human suffering. The ones we must, the ones we needn't and the ones we can optionally endure. Because, if we were able to master ourselves — and even the external effects imposed upon ourselves — it's at that point we can truly become the sovereign owners of ourselves and our purpose.

Every living creature comes into their lives with a hardwired set of prime directives. The absolutely base consideration of them all is that of survival. The survival instinct allows for the most necessary implementations of priority action to keep the individual alive. Above all things, don't die. This universal prerogative gives latitude to all other a priori necessities like food, shelter or procreation. Within the code of this base requirement is a metric that serves as a barometer of survivability. The unit of measure, when it comes to the survival instinct of a life form, is suffering. Suffering is even more important than flourishing. It acts as a measure of how far you are from safety or from doom. It compels you to eat, it informs you of damage, and it motivates you to improve any situation that could lead to your destruction. There *absolutely* are necessary amounts of suffering we must experience, for the same reason that in its absence we could destroy ourselves. Without pain, we wouldn't know about injuries. Think about leaning on a hot stove top. Without hunger, we may become malnourished unintentionally. Its presence can work as a guardrail to keep us within the optimal boundaries of survivability. But at times, there can become a convolution or unintentional overriding of our guardrails that leads to self-imposed and unnecessary suffering. Like software that alters the functionality of the hardware it's loaded onto, our psychology can usurp our biological imperatives and for the sake of short term mental comfort, lead towards long term suffering.

It's for these reasons that knowing who you are and being able to keep who you are in check (with constant internal auditing) is so very important. Because, much of what causes our own internal suffering tends to stem from the least audited parts of our psychology. And it usually isn't something that happens overnight. It's a gradual aggregation of small allowances for weakness in the moment that, brick by brick, build a monolith that can overpower our threshold against suffering. It could be a lack of restraint for unhealthy eating that leads to disease and depression. It could be a lack of personal boundaries that leads you into a position of abuse by those apt to take advantage of your good will. It could even be as unassuming as the continual acquisition of knowledge to the exclusion of action. The lists could go on and on, but the reasons for this type of suffering equate to the same issue — a lack of personal sovereignty. Whether knowingly or unknowingly, the more we allow ourselves the permission to forfeit our own say in these small decisions, the less we retain the sovereignty to do so in the future. What's worse, a comfort in doing so can lead to the propensity for outsourcing our sovereignty in general to outside interests. This equates to the giving up of freedoms spoken to in the previous chapter. As an abandonment in personal responsibility leads to a tendency towards the easiest solution (sometimes simply procrastination or an indifference to the problem), this can create a weakness that is apt to trade sovereignty for ease.

Paradoxically, by doing so, this predisposition for the quick and easy answer (usually foisted upon someone else to solve for the price of your say- so in the matter) so often only adds to suffering in your life. As you willingly lose control of the reins over your self, that vacuum of ownership will be filled by something else instead. Sometimes it's a person or a power structure, or sometimes it's a vice or a substance. For every time you relinquish a piece of your sovereignty, you simultaneously make a bet that whatever thing or entity you've handed it over to will be in line with who you are individually. And more often than not, they aren't. This is what leads headlong into that inner tension we spoke to in chapter twenty-three. The result of which will be perpetual psychological suffering.

The good news, in this case, is that you were the person who caused this to happen — either willingly or by abandonment of responsibility. Which means, you also have the ability to *undo* the same process you started. The bad news about the good news is that to rectify the damages of our irresponsibility that lead to suffering will, *itself*, require suffering. But like reclaiming the autonomy over a limb that became atrophied for lack of use, instead of gaining immediate comfort for long term suffering, you trade short term suffering for long term strength. This, again, is why the efforts necessary to learn who you are and retain sovereignty over it are so monumentally important. And in this sense, the suffering it takes to begin and maintain that process are not only vital, but preempt a much more detrimental psychological outcome if we don't.

There is another form of suffering that is not as obviously in our control, though it's much more obvious in its existence. If the former self imposed psychological suffering could be categorized as something we can undo, this form of suffering resides in a separate category of that which simply cannot. Were we to equate it to the nature and nurture sides of our personality, what we can cause and undo would be nurture, while what is determined and intrinsic would be nature. There are many different kinds and degrees of natural suffering that we have no say in. In fact, to speak to the Buddhist view of things, they would make up the majority of total suffering that we experience. Although, there's a unique way that view gets flipped that we'll cover as we look deeper into the issues. But these impositions of suffering that get projected upon you, by no fault of your own, can be extreme and sometimes all consuming. People who are raised in violence that they cannot escape from. Those who are born with physical burdens that limit and pain them. Anyone who has lost loved ones through tragedy. There are so many different and intense vectors of external suffering in the world, and so many of them are utterly outside our ability to prevent or undo. But these kinds of suffering require a totally different tact to avail them to your personal sovereignty. And this is where the insights of the Buddhists come back and speak to how.

In the Buddhist view of life, the only thing we can hope to control is the self. Any attempt to impose control outside of that is its own form of suffering. But then, how is one supposed to limit suffering (the primary objective of the philosophy) if most of its causal vectors come from outside of our control? There is another simple yet incredibly difficult solution to this critical consideration. Being stricken with suffering you did not cause and could not prevent, the only aspect of that scenario where you have any say in *is* your mind. The predominance of the mind in this view is both the singular answer and the universal solution. Many different sects of Buddhist monks will voluntarily cause themselves external suffering to learn how to find internal peace within it. And therein is the hack. It all comes back to personal sovereignty. This time though, not in the sense of prevention or disallowance of suffering, but in an acceptance of what cannot be changed and a resolution not to allow external suffering to control the internal self. It may be the harder of the two sides of sovereignty to enact and master. But that again speaks to the necessity of both knowing your-self and where you stand in your present abilities, as well as the continual quest to learn from and improve upon where they fall short.

Nowadays, certain public figures who've taken it upon them-selves to make these points clear and apparent have risen to preeminence in global human discourse. People like Jocko Willink, a former US Navy SEAL commander who preaches the importance of personal discipline and responsibility. US Marine turned fitness and mindset coach, David Goggins, who purposefully overtaxes and continually punishes his body beyond the point of failure to fortify and dominate his own mind. Even public intellectuals like Professor emeritus Jordan Peterson who writes and speaks extensively to the vital importance of self mastery; in the physical, social and psychological arenas. The commonality between all of these and others like them is the demonstration of dedicating yourself to becoming sovereign. They, each in their own ways, speak to everything that we've covered in this third portion's focus on purpose. Moreover, they show what is available to anyone willing to take up responsibility for themselves; the personal fulfillment and societal benefits that come from it and a vision of a better humanity built by those who do. Through the examples of exemplary, highly sovereign people we have, at our feet, living proof of what is possible as well as the route for which to take if we too are to do the same.

In the end, suffering is inevitable. But through the mastering of your mind it needn't be the arbiter of our destiny. Through the tireless, honest and painful efforts required in gaining and maintaining sovereignty of one's self, suffering in any form can be refashioned from an implement against us into an opportunity to perfect us. But the choice is ours. It will and always has been. But what more beautiful, meaningful and fulfilling adventure could there be than its pursuit? To be free, we must free ourselves. To cite Voltaire, "Man is free at the moment he wishes to be.".

Be curious. Be honest. Be yourself. Be sovereign.

EPILOGUE

As a final thought, though this expansive exploration has come to a close, it is my hope that instead of an ending it has sparked the beginning of a journey. One that continues forward in humility and childlike curiosity.

To close, I'll end with a quote from J.R.R. Tolkien's timeless classic, *The Fellowship of the Ring*:

"It's a dangerous business, Frodo, going out your door. You step onto the road, and if you don't keep your feet, there's no knowing where you might be swept off to."

— BILBO BAGGINS

May the roads you follow sweep you towards purpose and adventure.

~ **Drew Weatherhead**

Lightning Source UK Ltd.
Milton Keynes UK
UKHW040440240223
417573UK00002B/35